THE USBORNE BOOK OF
WORLD HISTORY

This book is an introduction to world history from the first
civilisations to the early 20th century. An understanding of other
people and their history is becoming vitally important in our
increasingly interdependent world, but many people find it
difficult to acquire an overall view of world history because they
have never had attractive enough starting points. This book
provides these in short visual chapters which describe, in simple
terms, the major developments in the history of the world. It is, of
course, immensely difficult to produce a world history, especially
when aiming at young readers, and controversial selections have
inevitably had to be made. This book does not attempt to be a
comprehensive account of the history of the world, however. A vast
amount of detail has been omitted, but there are suggestions at the
back of the book for finding out more, and every library, bookshop
and museum contains a wide variety of material which can take
the reader beyond the stimulating starting points this book
provides.

Contents

First published in 1985 by Usborne Publishing Ltd, Usborne House, 83-85 Saffron Hill, London, EC1N 8RT
Copyright © 2008, 1985 Usborne Publishing Ltd

The material in this book was originally published as six separate volumes with the Titles: The First Civilisations; Warriors & Seafarers; Empires & Barbarians; Crusaders, Aztecs, Samurai; Exploration & Discovery; The Age of Revolutions.

Consultant Editors: Brian Adams, Verulamium Museum, St Albans; D. Barass, University of East Anglia; Professor Edmund Bosworth, Dept of Near Eastern Studies, University of Manchester; Ben Burt, Museum of Mankind, London; Dr Warwick Bray, Elizabeth Carter, Mark Hassall, Amelie Kuhrt, Institute of Archaeology, London; Dr M. C. Chapman, University of Hull; T. R. Clayton, Norman Hampson, University of York; George Hart, British Museum, London; Dr C. J. Heywood, University of London; Dr Alan Johnston, Dept of Classical Archaeology, University College, London; Peter Johnson, Commonwealth Institute, London; Dr Michael Loewe, University of Cambridge; Dr M. McCauley, University of London; Dr Roger Moorey, Dept Antiquities, Ashmolean Museum, Oxford; Dr J. A. Sharpe, University of York; Dr C. D. Sheldon, University of Cambridge; R. W. Skelton, Victoria & Albert Museum, London; Margaret Somerville, Visiting Lecturer in Oriental Antiquites, British Museum, London; Joanna Strub, School of Oriental and African Studies, London; Dr R. Waller, University of Cambridge.

CHILDREN'S ENCYCLOPEDIA OF
HISTORY
FIRST CIVILISATIONS TO THE FALL OF ROME

Dr Anne Millard and Patricia Vanags

Illustrated by Joseph McEwan
Designed by Graham Round
Edited by Jenny Tyler

Digging up History

We find out about peoples of the past by looking at the remains of things they left behind them and reading the texts they wrote. Digging up these remains is called archaeology.

The exact position of objects in the ground is very important. Modern archaeologists work with great care and patience, digging their site in sections and recording each find, however small.

Buried cities

A site may be inhabited for thousands of years. New houses are built on the ruins of the old and rubbish piles up. Gradually a mound or "tell" is formed. The oldest things are at the bottom of the tell.

After capture the city was burnt and survivors carried away into slavery.

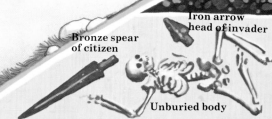
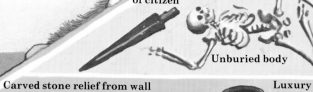

Iron arrow head of invader

Bronze spear of citizen

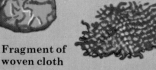

Unburied body

1250BC to 1200BC approximately. More and more weapons appeared as the situation with neighbours became desperate. Then the city was captured.

Carved stone relief from wall

Luxury goods of silver and gold

Carved ivory decoration from furniture

1500BC to 1250BC approximately. The town grew into a city. The people traded with foreign lands and became wealthy. They enjoyed a high standard of living, but needed huge defences to protect them from jealous neighbours.

Painting from house or temple wall

Local pottery

2000BC to 1500BC approximately. Nomads arrived and were gradually and peacefully absorbed into the community. Arts, crafts and learning flourished.

Ancient writing

The Rosetta Stone with text in Greek and Ancient Egyptian.

Scholars often spend years working out forgotten languages. This tablet was a lucky find. Its text was written in two languages, one of which was already known.

Town wall of huge stones

Tablet with picture writing

3000BC to 2000BC approximately. The village prospered and and became a town. A defensive wall was built. The inhabitants learnt how to make pottery and use copper and gold. They also began to write.

Copper fish hook

Carved stone statue

Mud brick huts

Stamp seal

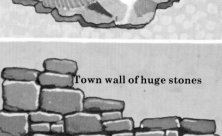

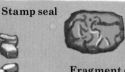

Human skull

Fragment of woven cloth

6000BC to 3000BC approximately. Early farmers settled down and built small huts. They had few possessions,

Animal bones

Flint tools

Stone Age people camped here. They left flint tools, their bones and bones of the animals they hunted.

Bedrock.

The letters BC mean "Before Christ". Dates with BC next to them are numbers of years before the birth of Christ.

Layer of sand and dirt.

The tell in this picture has been made up to give you an idea of how archaeologists can dig down through history. No real mound would have such flat regular layers. The objects are not drawn to scale.

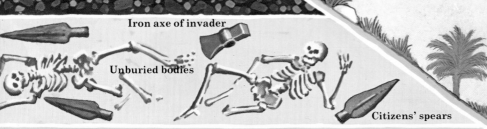

Iron axe of invader

Unburied bodies

Citizens' spears

Monumental gateway

Foreign pottery

Stone statue

Piles of tablets covered with text

Local pottery

Bronze sword

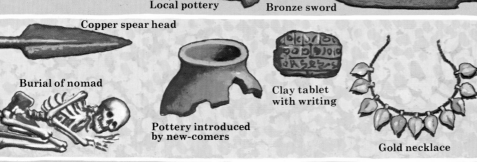

Copper spear head

Burial of nomad

Pottery introduced by new-comers

Clay tablet with writing

Gold necklace

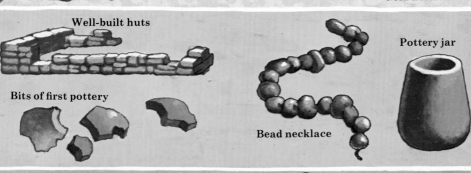

Well-built huts

Bits of first pottery

Bead necklace

Pottery jar

Stone jar

Stone figure of a goddess

Wooden bowl

Bones of tamed animals

Animal tusk

Human jawbone

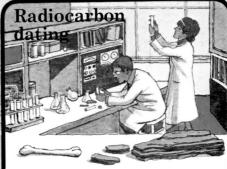

Radiocarbon dating

A living plant, such as a tree, absorbs a substance called radioactive carbon, or C14. After death, C14 slowly leaves the plant. By measuring how much C14 is left, scientists can work out when the tree died.

Tree-ring dating

Ring pattern on piece of old wood.

Every year a tree adds a ring round its trunk. Trees in the same area have the same pattern of rings. It is sometimes possible to make a chart of rings which goes back for centuries and use it for dating old wood.

Putting pieces together

Every fragment found on a dig is numbered and recorded. This chair was reconstructed because the position of every piece of gold foil was noted.

The First Settlers

Around 10,000BC, our ancestors gathered plants, hunted and fished for their food. They were nomads, wandering from place to place after the herds they hunted. Sometimes, though, a good supply of game or fish meant they could settle in one place for a while.

Rush basket

Drying skin

Leather skirt

Wolf-tooth necklace

Fishing net

Cleaning animal skin with flint scraper.

Stone tools

Carving an antler

Some Stone Age people made their homes in the caves of northern Europe. They made their tools from stone, wood and bone, and their clothes from animal skins.

The children were told stories of the past by the old people of the tribe. Their fathers hunted and fished and their mothers gathered berries and plants.

1 Learning to farm

Gradually people realized that seeds dropped on the ground grew into plants. They began to plant seeds specially, breaking up the hard ground first to help them grow.

2

By choosing the best seeds, they grew better plants and got a bigger harvest. This food supply was more reliable than hunting, so many people settled down to farm.

3

MEDITERRANEAN SEA

Wild wheat

Wild barley

Barley areas
Wheat areas

This discovery must have taken place in the Middle East where the ancestors of wheat and barley grew wild. Later, other plants and vegetables were planted.

Taming animals

About the same time as they learnt how to plant crops, people began to tame animals. They tamed sheep and goats first and then cattle, pigs and donkeys. This meant they had a supply of meat, milk, wool and animals for carrying loads.

Building houses

People settled where the land was good for farming. If there were no caves nearby, they had to build homes for themselves from whatever materials were available locally. They built a style of house to suit the climate.

New crafts

Reed basket

Spinning

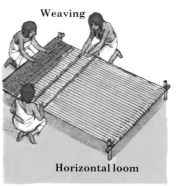

Weaving

Horizontal loom

Sewing with a bone needle.

Staying in one place and farming, gave people more spare time. They improved old skills, like weaving reeds into baskets and mats, and developed new ones like spinning and pottery. This may have been discovered by accident when a clay-lined basket fell into a fire.

With the wool from their tame sheep and goats, people discovered how to spin and weave and make cloth. They also found they could make linen cloth from the fibres of the flax plant. Needles made from bone were used to sew pieces of cloth together to make garments.

Early pottery

Pot decorated with scratched pattern.

Rough cooking pots were probably made by women, but in settlements which could afford to support them, potters were able to spend all day making good quality pots.

Make a simple loom

Use a piece of card about 20cm × 12cm. Cut little triangles out of the ends to make "teeth". Then wind wool round the card to make the "warp". Weave "weft" wool in and out of the warp. You can join different colours with a knot.

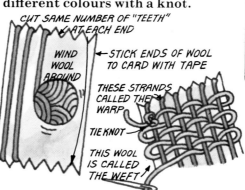

CUT SAME NUMBER OF "TEETH" AT EACH END

WIND WOOL AROUND

← STICK ENDS OF WOOL TO CARD WITH TAPE

THESE STRANDS CALLED THE WARP

TIE KNOT

THIS WOOL IS CALLED THE WEFT

Using metal

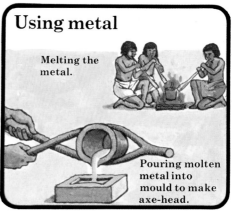

Melting the metal.

Pouring molten metal into mould to make axe-head.

Our ancestors had been settled for thousands of years before they discovered how to use metals. Copper, gold and silver were used first. Then bronze was discovered.

Jericho

Near the modern city of Jericho lie the remains of one of the oldest towns in the world. Archaeologists have found some other very old sites in the Middle East, but these are only villages.

TURKEY

Çatal Hüyük

MEDITERRANEAN SEA

Jericho

River Nile

RED SEA

SINAI

1 A town grows

Some time after 10,000 BC a group of hunters, attracted by a good supply of food and water, settled on the site which was to become the town of Jericho.

2

*Cut-away wall

By about 8000 BC, they were living in a village and had probably begun to farm, though they had not learned how to make pottery. They buried their dead under their houses.

3

As they became more wealthy, their village grew into a town. To protect themselves against jealous neighbours, they built a stone wall with towers and a ditch round it.

4

Jericho's wealth must have come from trade. Local goods such as salt and bitumen were traded for obsidian from Turkey, cowrie shells from the Red Sea and turquoise from Sinai.

5

*Cut-away wall

Grinding corn

Despite the defences, Jericho must have been captured. By about 7000 BC, new people, who built rectangular houses instead of round ones, were living there.

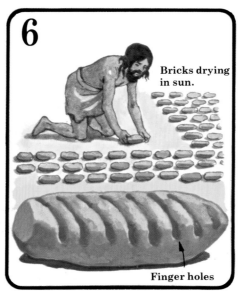

6

Bricks drying in sun.

Finger holes

The houses in Jericho were built of mud bricks. These were moulded by hand and left to dry in the sun. This kind of brick is still used in dry places.

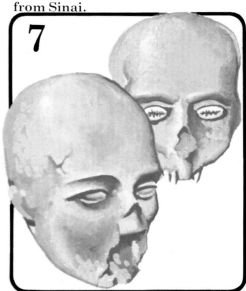

7

Skulls like these, with faces modelled in plaster and shell eyes, were dug up at Jericho. Scholars suggest people made them to show respect for their dead ancestors.

* In these pictures, we have removed some of the wall so you can see inside.

Çatal Hüyük

Of all the ancient settlements found so far, the largest is Çatal Hüyük (pronounced Chatal Hooyuk). Excavations show that it flourished between 6500 BC and 5650 BC.

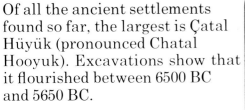

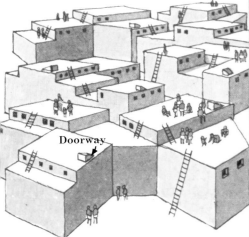

Doorway

The houses were one storey high. People entered them by climbing a ladder and crawling through a hole in the roof. This meant it was difficult for enemies to get in.

Obsidian mirror

Steps to doorway

Obsidian daggers

Carved wooden dish

Stove

Sleeping platform (the dead were buried under here)

The houses had one main room. Benches and sleeping platforms were built in to the walls and woven mats covered the floor. The people of Çatal Hüyük used the obsidian, or volcanic glass, found nearby for making daggers and mirrors and traded them for flint and shells.

Statue of Catal Hüyük goddess.

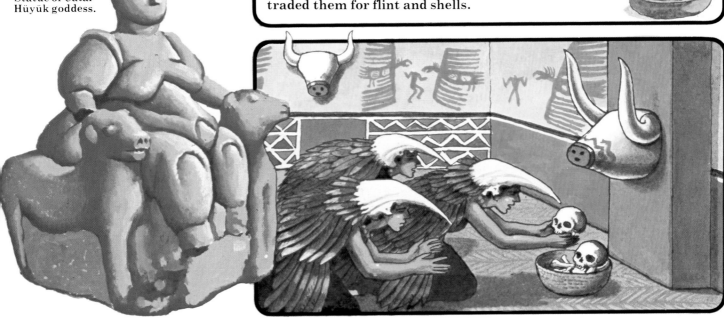

The Çatal Hüyük people worshipped a goddess who is shown as a girl, a mother or an old woman. They also worshipped a god whose sacred animal was a bull.

Many shrines have been found at Çatal Hüyük. Their walls were brightly painted with religious scenes and decorated with plaster bulls' heads with real horns.

Wall paintings suggest that some priestesses dressed as vultures and conducted rituals. Skulls were found in baskets below the bulls' heads.

The First Great Civilisation

Some 7,000 years ago, farmers began to move into the area between the Tigris and Euphrates rivers and settle there. This area was later called "Mesopotamia" by the Ancient Greeks, which means "The land between two rivers". It is roughly where Iraq is now.

Life was hard there. The weather was hot and dry and the rivers flooded, but the land was fertile when properly looked after. Gradually, in the south in the land of Sumer, a great civilisation grew up.

Map of Sumer

The land of Sumer where the Sumerians lived was in the southern part of Mesopotamia. The land near the Persian Gulf was very marshy and difficult to farm, but there were plenty of fish and wild fowl there for the settlers to eat. To the north of Sumer was the land which later became called Akkad.

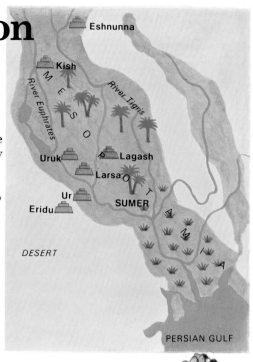

 City-states

 Marshy land

Sumer had no stone or tall trees for building. The first houses there were built with reeds. The Marsh Arabs who live in the area today still build reed houses.

The two rivers flooded in early summer. The Sumerians built a system of irrigation canals to water their fields and drain the land.

Later, the Sumerians built their houses of sun-dried mud bricks. These mud-brick buildings kept them cool in summer and warm in winter.

Every village was under the protection of a god or goddess who lived in a temple built on a platform. The priests of the temple became very powerful and important.

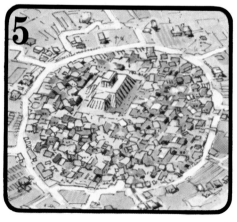

The Sumerian villages grew into self-governing city-states which were huge walled cities, with a temple at the centre and farmland all around.

Sometimes one city-state conquered another and ruled it for a while, but no one king ever made himself ruler of the whole of Sumer, let alone Mesopotamia.

How we know

An inlaid box was found at Ur. It is called the "Battle Standard", but it may have been part of a musical instrument. It shows scenes of life in peacetime on one side and scenes of war on the other.

From this we learn what Sumerian warriors, weapons and chariots looked like. The Sumerians did not have horses, so the chariots were pulled by donkeys or wild asses called onagers.

We can get some idea of what the Sumerians looked like and what clothes they wore from statues found in their temples. Nobles or priests seem to have shaved their heads.

The ziggurat of Ur

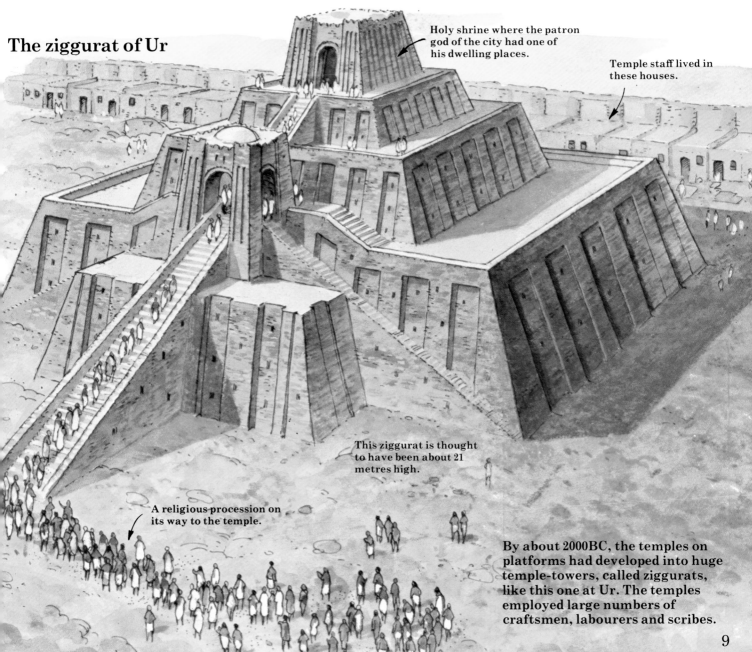

Holy shrine where the patron god of the city had one of his dwelling places.

Temple staff lived in these houses.

This ziggurat is thought to have been about 21 metres high.

A religious procession on its way to the temple.

By about 2000BC, the temples on platforms had developed into huge temple-towers, called ziggurats, like this one at Ur. The temples employed large numbers of craftsmen, labourers and scribes.

9

The Invention of Writing

1

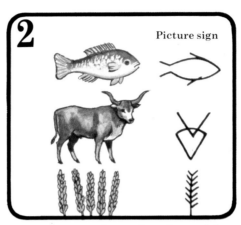

This stone vase records offerings made to the goddess Inanna at Ur.

The Sumerian temples collected gifts for the gods and goddesses and also handed out goods as payments. As the Sumerians' wealth grew, a simple system of keeping accounts became necessary.

2

Picture sign

They began to draw sketches of the objects they wished to record using a flattened piece of clay and a reed pen. This is the earliest form of writing.

3

At first, the pictures were drawn underneath each other on the wet clay. The clay was then dried in the sun or baked in a kiln to make it into a hard tablet.

4

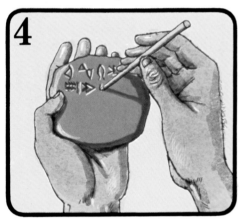

Later, scribes found that it was easier to draw the signs sideways. As time passed, the pictures they drew were less and less like the objects they represented.

5

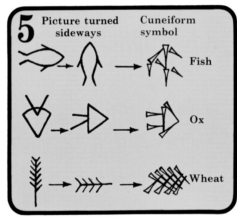

Picture turned sideways — Cuneiform symbol

Fish
Ox
Wheat

Because of the shape of the reed pen, the pictures were turned into wedge-shaped symbols. We call this kind of writing cuneiform, which means "wedge-shaped".

6

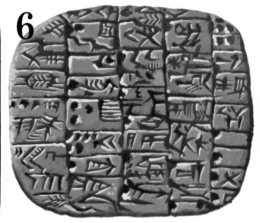

By adapting the signs and using them together, other words could be built up. This meant they could write sentences expressing ideas as well as list objects.

Sumerian schools

Those who could afford to, sent their sons to school. School began very early and lasted until evening. The boys had to take lunch with them and work very hard.

Assistant master — Apprentice teacher — Headmaster — Boys reciting a lesson — Bowl containing wet clay for tablets.

Reading, writing and arithmetic were taught in the schools. Discipline was very strict and boys were beaten for not doing their lessons properly.

One Sumerian story tells of a schoolmaster being bribed. A boy got a good report by persuading his father to give the master presents.

A Sumerian market

Sumer had no metal, stone or timber so all these things had to be imported from other countries.

This scribe checks that the right amount of goods is being unloaded.

Writing made the daily business of buying and selling in the markets much easier. If a dispute arose over a deal, the written contract could be checked.

Timber imported from the Middle East.

This trader can keep an account of the amount he is owed for his skins.

Sealing a contract with a cylinder seal.

People who could not write hired public scribes to write letters for them.

Cylinder seals

Carved stone seal

Impression of seal in clay

Instead of signing their names, the Sumerians used cylinder seals, which they rolled across the wet clay. No two seals were alike, so the owner could always be identified.

Measuring and calculating

Scribes measured the land to see how much tax the farmers had to pay. The fields were divided into equal squares for this and then the number of squares were counted up.

The Sumerians used two counting systems. One was a decimal system, like ours, based on the unit 10. The other, based on units of 60, is still in use today for measuring time.

Your own picture writing

You can make picture signs with a sharp pencil on a flattened piece of plasticine. You could make up a system of picture writing and use it to write messages to your friends.

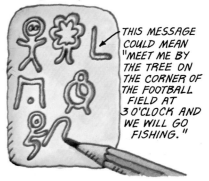

THIS MESSAGE COULD MEAN "MEET ME BY THE TREE ON THE CORNER OF THE FOOTBALL FIELD AT 3 O'CLOCK AND WE WILL GO FISHING."

11

Daily Life

The Sumerians thought that their city-states were owned by the local gods and goddesses. They divided the land into three parts and farmed one part of it for the gods. This produce was stored and used in times of famine or traded for goods from abroad.

The second part of the land produced food for the priests and temple staff. The third was hired by the citizens to grow food for themselves. They paid their rent with some of the crop.

A nobleman at home

The king ran the city-state on behalf of the gods, with the help of priests, scribes and nobles. Some of these were very rich and enjoyed a good life.

This gaming board comes from one of the royal graves of Ur. The rules are not known, though recently a way of playing it has been worked out.

A rich merchant's house

Bedroom

Servant girl

Ladles and strainers

Kitchen

Water jars

Fire for cooking   Reed mat

To lavatory

Grinding flour

Master's bedroom

Wash bowl and jug

Servants' room

Spinning

Built-in mud bench

Archaeologists found large two storey houses, like this one, at Ur. They were built of mud bricks round open courtyards. They had lavatories and drains, but not baths apparently. Houses like this probably belonged to merchants who were wealthy, but whose status was beneath that of the priests and nobles.

Most ordinary Sumerians lived in small, one storey houses built of sun-dried mud bricks. Windows, when they had them, were small to keep out heat and cold.

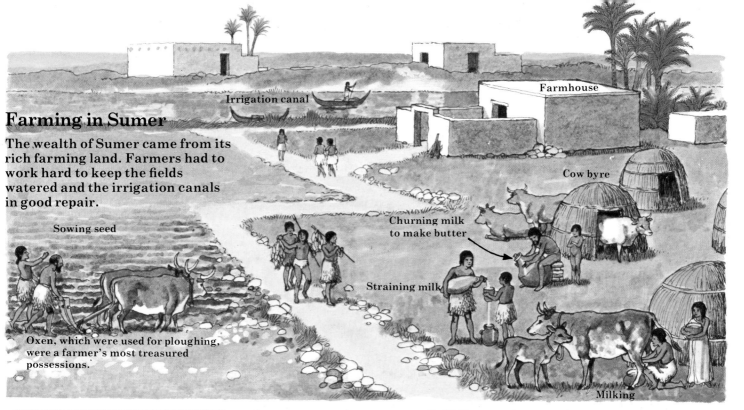

Farming in Sumer

The wealth of Sumer came from its rich farming land. Farmers had to work hard to keep the fields watered and the irrigation canals in good repair.

Irrigation canal

Farmhouse

Cow byre

Churning milk to make butter

Sowing seed

Straining milk

Oxen, which were used for ploughing, were a farmer's most treasured possessions.

Milking

The first wheels

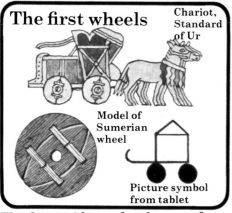

Chariot, Standard of Ur

Model of Sumerian wheel

Picture symbol from tablet

The first evidence for the use of wheels comes from Sumer. Sumerian wheels were made from three pieces of wood, lashed together.

Potters at work

Clay being mixed

Kilns

Pots drying out before baking

Potter's wheel

Though stone and wood were scarce in Sumer, there was plenty of mud and clay which could be used to make pottery. So much pottery was needed that skilled potters worked full time.

Metalwork

Sumerian metalsmiths were skilled workers in gold, silver and copper. The things they made were expensive because all Sumer's metal had to be imported.

The royal graves of Ur

This gold jewellery comes from one of the royal graves of Ur. These graves contain the skeletons of dozens of people who appear to have committed suicide in order to follow the graves' owners to another world.

Key dates

5000	Early farming communities using pottery living in northern Mesopotamia.
4000	Communities established in the south, in Sumer. The Ubaid period.
3300/2800	Rapid development of the civilisation of Sumer.
2750	The Royal Graves of Ur.
2700	**Gilgamesh** reigned at Uruk. 1st Dynasty (line of hereditary rulers) at Ur.
2500	2nd Dynasty at Ur.

Approximate BC dates

First Settlers on the Nile

1

Thousands of years ago, the Sahara was a well-watered plain where wild animals lived. Stone Age people lived there too and hunted the animals.

2

Slowly the climate changed and the Sahara became a desert. People and animals had to search for a water supply. Some of them reached the land we call Egypt.

3

In these times, the valley of the River Nile was a marshy jungle where dangerous animals lived. The new comers camped on the edges of the valley for safety.

4

After a while, the hunters learnt to tame animals rather than hunt and kill them. They domesticated dogs, cattle, sheep, pigs, goats and donkeys.

5

The number of people grew and they were able to clear land near the river and build villages there. They found out how to plant seeds and grew wheat barley and vegetables. They also discovered how to make pottery, spin and weave flax to make linen clothes and use metals like copper and gold to make tools and weapons.

6

Before the inundation

During the inundation

Every year, in July, flood waters from the south burst the Nile's banks and soaked the hard, dry ground. The flood lasted several weeks and was called the inundation.

7

The Ancient Egyptians discovered how to save enough of this flood water to last the whole year. They cut canals and ditches which stored the water and carried it to the fields.

Egypt becomes one land

8

Gradually communities in the Nile Valley joined together. By 3200BC, Egypt had just two kings—one in Lower Egypt and one in Upper Egypt. Then they fought a battle which was won by Upper Egypt.

9

A new capital was built for the united land at Memphis. As ruler of The Two Lands, the king wore the Double Crown. He also carried the Crook and Flail to show he was shepherd and defender of his people.

The name "Narmer"

The god, Horus, helping Narmer.

Defeated ruler of Lower Egypt.

King Narmer wearing his White Crown.

Beheaded enemies.

King Narmer wearing the Red Crown.

Here you can see the two sides of King Narmer's palette. The pictures carved on it show Narmer, King of Upper Egypt, defeating the King of Lower Egypt and claiming to be king of the whole land.

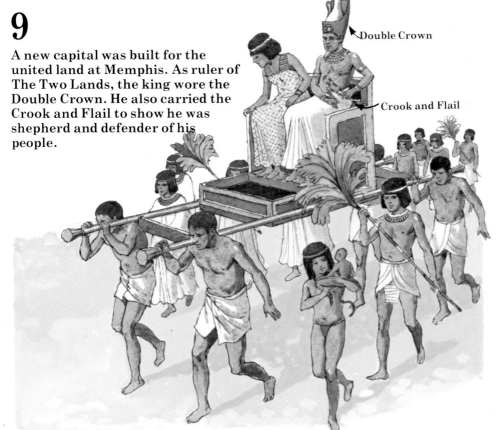

Double Crown

Crook and Flail

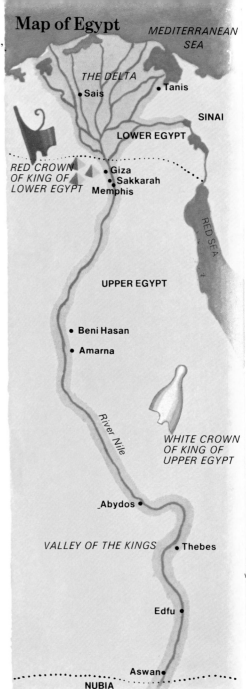

Map of Egypt

MEDITERRANEAN SEA

THE DELTA

• Sais   • Tanis

SINAI

LOWER EGYPT

RED CROWN OF KING OF LOWER EGYPT

• Giza
• Sakkarah
Memphis

RED SEA

UPPER EGYPT

• Beni Hasan

• Amarna

River Nile

WHITE CROWN OF KING OF UPPER EGYPT

Abydos •

VALLEY OF THE KINGS   • Thebes

Edfu •

Aswan •

NUBIA

Egypt is a long, narrow and very fertile country. In the north, the country widens into the area known as the Delta. This map shows the borders between Upper and Lower Egypt before the country was united in about 3120BC.

The king's name

The Egyptians thought it rude to refer directly to the king, so they spoke of "The Great House". The picture signs, or hieroglyphs, for this in Egyptian writing are:

which is pronounced "per-o". The word "pharaoh" which we use for Egyptian kings comes from this.

The Farmers' Year

1 In July, the waters of the Nile began to rise. The land flooded and animals had to be moved to higher ground.

2 By November the water had gone down. The damp earth was broken up with digging sticks, ploughed and sown with seed.

3 Egypt has very little rain. The fields were watered with flood waters which had been stored in canals.

4 The crops grew during the winter. Tax officials measured the crop and decided how much of it the farmer must pay as tax.

5 The crop was harvested in the spring. The farmer's family helped with this.

6 Cattle were used to separate the grain from the stalks. The grain was tossed so the husks would blow away.

7 The grain was stored in the granaries in huge bins called silos. The scribes checked that none of it was stolen.

8 The irrigation canals and ditches then had to be repaired and made ready for the next flood.

9 During the inundation, some farmers worked on the pharaoh's building projects. This was part of the tax they owed him.

Food and Drink

It was the prayer of all Egyptians that, in the Next World, they would have all the good things to eat and drink that they had known in life.

The Nile provided much of their food. They used nets to trap wild ducks, geese and other water birds that lived in the reeds and caught many kinds of fish from the river.

Birds were also raised on farms where they were forcibly fattened for the table, like the stork in this picture. The eggs of these birds were eaten too.

Meat

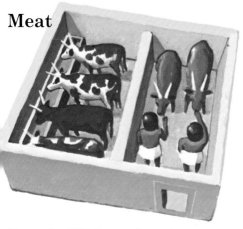

Egypt had little good pasture, so cattle raised for meat were often fattened in stalls. This wooden model of a cow stall came from an Egyptian tomb at Thebes.

Wine-making

Grapes were grown on trellises. To make them into wine, they were put into troughs and the juice trodden out. The treaders clung to ropes to stop them slipping.

Wine jars had inscriptions on them saying where the wine came from and when it was produced. These are often valuable as historical evidence.

Bread

Wheat and barley were ground into flour between two stones. To make bread dough, the flour was mixed with water.

Flavourings, such as garlic or honey, were added to the dough. Then it was packed into clay pots and baked in a fire.

Beer

Some loaves were only lightly baked, then mixed with water and passed through a sieve to make beer.

The beer often needed straining before it was drunk and special pottery strainers were made for the purpose.

17

Tombs and Life after Death

1 Death of a nobleman

When, despite the efforts of the doctors and the prayers of the priests, an Egyptian noble died, his body had to be embalmed to prevent it from decaying.

2

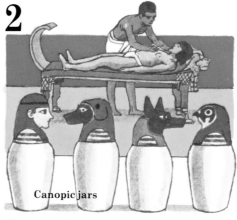

Canopic jars

First, the brain and internal organs were removed and placed in special "canopic" jars. The body was then treated with a substance called natron to help preserve it.

3

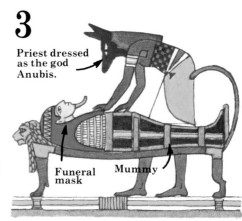

Priest dressed as the god Anubis.

Funeral mask   Mummy

The preserved body was wrapped in many layers of linen bandages, and a funeral mask put over its face. We often call a body embalmed like this a "mummy".

Mastaba tombs

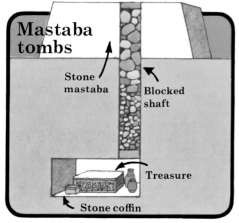

Stone mastaba

Blocked shaft

Treasure

Stone coffin

In the Old Kingdom (2686 to 2181BC), noblemen were buried under great rectangular stone tombs called mastabas. Some contained rooms decorated with scenes of daily life.

The pyramids

Kings of the Old and Middle Kingdoms of Egypt (2686 to 1633BC) were buried under huge stone pyramids. There are more than 30 pyramids in Egypt, but the most famous are the ones in Giza, shown here, where three kings and their chief queens were buried. Originally these pyramids were encased in gleaming white limestone, but this has now disappeared.

The sphinx, which guards the pyramids of Giza, was one of the forms of the Egyptian sun god. Its face is possibly a likeness of the pharaoh Khafra.

Poor people's graves

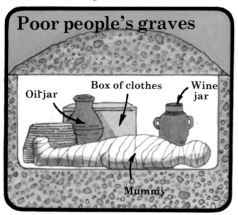

Oil jar   Box of clothes   Wine jar

Mummy

Poor people were buried in holes in the sand. Loving relatives supplied the best they could afford to make the dead person comfortable in the Next World.

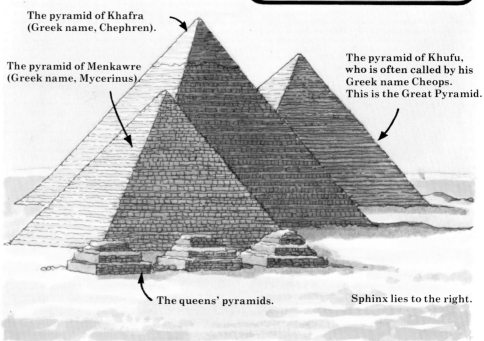

The pyramid of Khafra (Greek name, Chephren).

The pyramid of Menkawre (Greek name, Mycerinus).

The pyramid of Khufu, who is often called by his Greek name Cheops. This is the Great Pyramid.

The queens' pyramids.   Sphinx lies to the right.

4

Embalming took 70 days. After that the funeral could take place. Mourners, priests and grave goods accompanied the coffin across the Nile and to the tomb.

5

Man's widow

The last rites were performed at the tomb door. The "Opening of the Mouth" ceremony gave back to the dead person the power to eat, breathe and move.

6

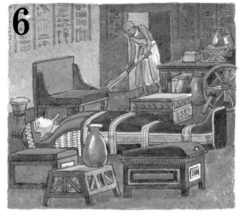

Everything the dead man needed in the Next World was placed in the burial chamber. The priests then left, sweeping away their footprints as they went.

Isis

Osiris, god of the dead.

Thoth, scribe of the gods.

Horus leading dead man.

Dead man's heart

Anubis

The Egyptians believed the souls of the dead were ferried across a river into the Next World. There they had to answer questions about their actions on earth. To help them, the priests wrote the Book of the Dead, which told them what to say and do. In the presence of Osiris, god of the dead, the person's heart was weighed against a feather representing truth. If the scales balanced the person had led a good life and went to eternal joy. If the heart was heavy with sin, a monster gobbled it up.

Building the Pyramids

The pyramids of Giza are one of the wonders of the world They were built without machines. The men who built them were not slaves, but peasant farmers who laboured for the king during the inundation and were paid for their services in food, oil and cloth. They probably hoped that by helping with the king's preparations for death, they would please the gods and be rewarded in the Next World.

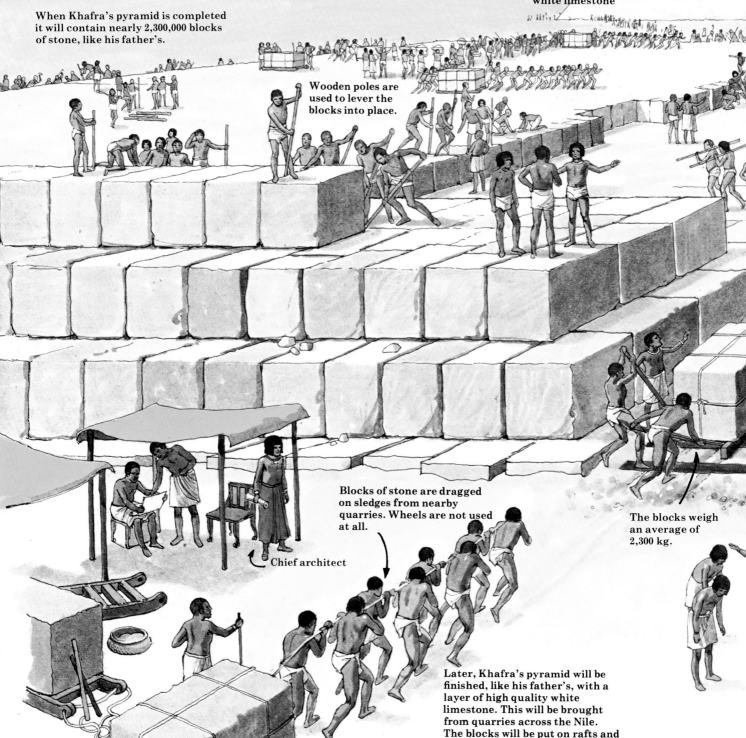

Khufu's pyramid

The height of Khufu's pyramid is 148m.

Casing of gleaming white limestone

When Khafra's pyramid is completed it will contain nearly 2,300,000 blocks of stone, like his father's.

Wooden poles are used to lever the blocks into place.

Chief architect

Blocks of stone are dragged on sledges from nearby quarries. Wheels are not used at all.

The blocks weigh an average of 2,300 kg.

Later, Khafra's pyramid will be finished, like his father's, with a layer of high quality white limestone. This will be brought from quarries across the Nile. The blocks will be put on rafts and floated across the river while it is in flood.

The year is 2565BC. The pyramid of King Khufu has been completed and his son Khafra is now reigning. Work on Khafra's pyramid has just begun. It will take at least 20 years to complete.

Khufu's queens' pyramids

Workmen's village

Inside the pyramid of Khufu

Burial chamber

Despite their great size, the pyramids contained only a few corridors and a burial chamber. In this lay the king's body in its stone sarcophagus.

Overseer

Ramps of rubble are used to raise the block. These will be removed when the building is finished.

The vizier, who is the king's chief minister, comes to inspect the work.

Valley of the Kings on the west bank at Thebes.

Later tombs

Paintings showing scenes from person's life

Sealed passage

Coffin

In the New Kingdom (1567 to 1085BC), the kings were buried in rock-cut tombs in a hidden valley on the west bank at Thebes. Great treasures were buried with them.

Inside Tutankhamun's tomb.

Tutankhamun was a boy-king who was buried in the smallest tomb in the Valley of the Kings. It alone escaped the tomb robbers and its treasure found intact.

Mask of Tutankhamun

Sport and Leisure

Painted wooden pillars

These children are playing a kind of tug-of-war.

These men are playing a board game rather like draughts.

Lyre

Harp

Young dancing girls

Wrestlers

This is the garden of a rich Egyptian. Most people who owned land made themselves shady gardens to sit in. Singing, music and dancing were favourite entertainments. We have no written music from Ancient Egypt, but the words of some songs have survived and also some of the musical instruments.

Children's games

Child's basket of toys from a tomb.

Ivory dog

Egyptian tomb paintings, like these, show us some of the games played by children, but they do not tell us the rules. They are often shown playing ball games. The balls they used were made of leather, stuffed with grain.

If a child died, toys were buried with him, like those in the basket above. Toys with moving parts were popular. This ivory hound opens and shuts its mouth as if to bark when a rod underneath is pressed.

Hunting on the Nile

Tame birds were held up to attract the wild ones.

Egyptian noblemen hunted and fished in the marshes using small boats made of papyrus stems bound together. They speared fish and used throwing sticks to bring down water birds.

Some had hunting cats, which were trained to retrieve the fallen birds. A man often took his family on these expeditions too, and they had a picnic on their boat.

Egyptian cosmetics

Both men and women used cosmetics. Oils and perfumes were used on the skin, the lips were painted red, and green and grey kohl was used to outline the eyes. Kohl was made from finely ground minerals mixed with oil.

Highly polished silver mirror

Cosmetic box

Perfume jar

Cosmetic jars

Hippo hunt

One of the most dangerous animals in Egypt was the hippopotamus. To hunt it, several skilled men were needed, armed with harpoons, spears, ropes and nets.

Water tournament

The object of this competition was to knock the crew of the rival boat into the water, one by one, without being toppled in yourself.

Key dates

5000	First traces of farming communities in Egypt.
4000/3500	Farmers prospered, communities grew and united.
3118	Upper and Lower Egypt united by **Menes,** first king of Dynasty I.
2686	**The Old Kingdom.** Beginning of Dynasty III. Step pyramid built.
2613	Dynasty IV. Giza pyramids built.
2180	End of Old Kingdom. Time of civil war and anarchy called First Intermediate Period.
2040	Egypt reunited. **The Middle Kingdom** A period of great prosperity during Dynasties XI to XIII.
1720	The Hyksos invaded. Second Intermediate Period.
1567	Egypt reunited and the Hyksos driven out.

Approximate BC dates

A Great Island Civilisation

The descendants of farmers who settled on the island of Crete were free from invasion for hundreds of years. This meant they could develop a distinctive way of life of their own.

We call the culture of the people of Crete "Minoan" after King Minos who is said to have ruled there. Many Minoan sites have been identified and excavated.

1

Silver hairpin with Linear A signs.

The Minoans sometimes used a system of hieroglyphs, or picture signs, for writing. They also had a script called Linear A which has not yet been deciphered.

Besides wheat, barley, vegetables and grapes, the farmers grew large quantities of olives. The olives in this picture were dug up on Crete and are 3,400 years old.

3

This fresco shows a Cretan fisherman with his catch of fresh mackerel. As they lived close to the sea, fish was an important part of the people's diet.

4

Cretan cooking pots of pottery and bronze have been found, though fish were probably grilled on sticks over a fire. Oil from crushed olives was used in Cretan cooking.

Houses

Small pieces of glazed pottery like this one give us an idea of what Minoan town houses looked like. They were probably used as decorations on furniture.

Frescoes

Houses and palaces were decorated with frescoes like these. A fresco is a picture painted on the plaster of a wall while the plaster is still damp.

How to make a fresco

The skill in fresco painting is working quickly and accurately. You cannot correct any mistakes. To make a "fresco", mix some plaster of Paris and pour it into a foil dish. When it is firm, but still damp, paint on it with water paints.

The palace at Knossos

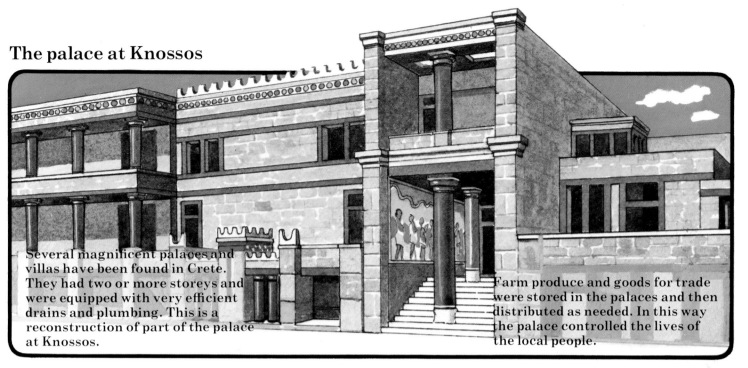

Several magnificent palaces and villas have been found in Crete. They had two or more storeys and were equipped with very efficient drains and plumbing. This is a reconstruction of part of the palace at Knossos.

Farm produce and goods for trade were stored in the palaces and then distributed as needed. In this way the palace controlled the lives of the local people.

The rooms in Minoan palaces were covered with bright frescoes. This is one of the queen's rooms in the palace of Knossos.

These large jars are called pithoi. They once held grain, wine and olive oil in the storage rooms of the palace of Knossos. They were found during excavations in 1900.

This throne, found at Knossos, is the oldest throne in Europe still standing in place. The decorations were probably done by Mycenaeans who occupied the palace for a while.

Life on Crete

Trade

The Cretans made beautiful pottery which is very easy to identify. The progress of Cretan traders is shown by the presence of this pottery on many sites.

According to tradition the Cretans were daring sailors and successful traders. The sailors of the legendary King Minos were said to rule the Mediterranean Sea.

The Egyptians recorded the arrival of Cretan traders in their tombs. They are shown carrying objects similar to those actually found on Minoan sites.

Games and Sports

No-one now knows the rules of the game once played on this board. It is known as the royal gaming board. Dice seem to have been a popular Minoan game.

This picture of boys boxing is based on a fresco found on the wall of a buried house on the nearby island of Thera. Note that each boy wears only one glove.

Frescoes and models show that Cretans enjoyed a dangerous sport known as bull-leaping. Highly trained young men and girls somersaulted between the horns of a charging bull. They worked in teams of three. One leaping, one catching and one ready for the next leap. Bull-leaping may have been a way of honouring the gods.

Religion and legend

Although they worshipped some gods, the leading role in Cretan religion was played by goddesses and their priestesses.

Gold and ivory statuette of a popular Cretan goddess.

1 This picture, which is from a seal impression, shows the goddess who was Queen of the Animals, standing on her mountain. In the background is a building which may be a shrine.

2 Cretans probably enjoyed dancing for its own sake, but it was also part of their way of worship. One legend tells how the craftsman Daedalus made a special dancing floor for the princess Ariadne.

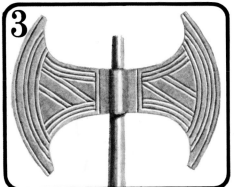

3 The Double Axe was a religious symbol. It appears as a decoration in frescoes and on various objects. Actual axes have also been found. This one is made of gold.

Legend says a terrible monster, the Minotaur, lived on Crete. It was half-bull and half-man and it lived in the Labyrinth. The hero Theseus found a way in and killed it.

The fall of Crete

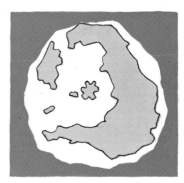

Thera was a small, round island some 70 miles north of Crete. About 1500BC, a gigantic volcanic eruption blew much of the island away. The white area on the map shows the land that sank beneath the sea.

The houses were completely buried under a thick layer of lava and ash, which preserved their walls to an unusual height. Modern excavations are now revealing the houses, their frescoes and other contents.

Some scholars think tidal waves and ash falls caused by the Thera eruption hit Crete and did so much damage that it never recovered. Invaders from Greece, the Mycenaeans, arrived and ruled at Knossos for a while, but the glory of Crete was past.

Key dates

6000/5000	Farmers living in settled communities.
4000	Beginning of metalworking. Evidence of gradually increasing prosperity.
2500/1950	Early Minoan Period. Towns developing.
1950	Middle Minoan Period. First palaces built. Picture writing (hieroglyphs) in use.
1700	Late Minoan Period. Great wealth and art. Palaces expanded.
1500	Eruption on nearby island of Thera. The arrival of the Mycenaeans. Linear B writing in use.
1200	Many sites abandoned.

Approximate BC dates

Cities of Ancient India

As in Mesopotamia and Egypt, people were drawn to the Indus Valley because of the river. The river meant that there was good farming land and a steady supply of fish. Goods could be carried more easily by river than across land.

It was not known until 1921 that a great and ancient civilisation had once existed in the Indus Valley. Much has been learnt about its people since then, but there are still many puzzles to be solved, perhaps by further excavations.

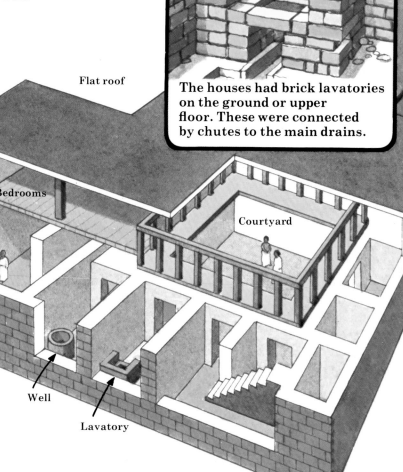

Very few statues of the Indus people have been found. This one may be of a priest. Skeletons from Harappa show that most people died before they were 40.

A street in Mohenjo-daro

Covered drain

Cities like Mohenjo-daro and Harappa were carefully planned with long, straight main streets linked by smaller lanes. Good drains ran down the main streets.

Clay missiles

Mohenjo-daro was protected by brick walls and towers. Piles of large clay missiles were left behind the walls ready for use, perhaps, as ammunition for slings.

Inside an Indus Valley house

The citizens of the Indus Valley cities lived in pleasant mud brick houses, built around courtyards. In a rich man's house, like this one, there was a well.

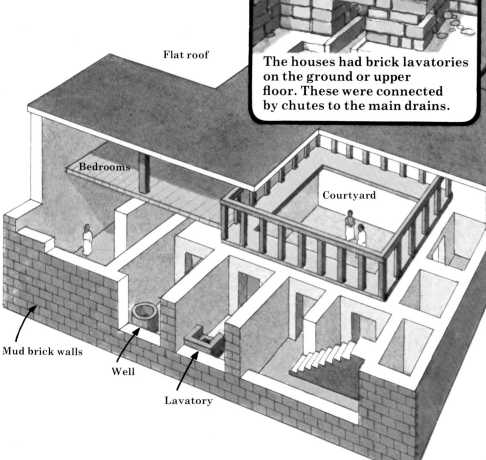

The houses had brick lavatories on the ground or upper floor. These were connected by chutes to the main drains.

Flat roof

Bedrooms

Courtyard

Mud brick walls

Well

Lavatory

Writing

Many seals have been found which show that the Indus people could write, but, as yet, no-one has been able to read the script. They were were probably used to stamp clay seals with the name of the owner.

Make a stamp seal

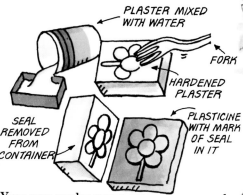

PLASTER MIXED WITH WATER

FORK

HARDENED PLASTER

SEAL REMOVED FROM CONTAINER

PLASTICINE WITH MARK OF SEAL IN IT

You can make your own stamp seal by mixing plaster with water and pouring it into a small container (1). Let it dry, then carve pictures on it with a fork (2). Turn out your seal and use it to make your special mark on a piece of plasticine (3).

Trade

Metal to make statues like this was bought from other countries. We know the Indus people traded in Mesopotamia because their pottery has been found there.

Granary at Mohenjo-daro

The granary was one of the most important buildings in the city. Farming was the chief source of wealth. The Indus people grew wheat, barley and vegetables and seem to have been the first people to grow cotton. Several other large buildings, including a great bath, have also been found.

How we know

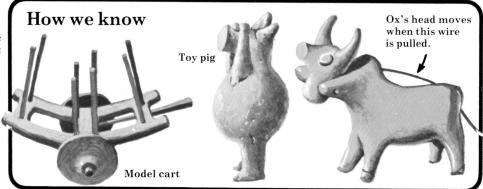

Toy pig

Ox's head moves when this wire is pulled.

Model cart

These models made of baked clay are valuable archaeological evidence. They were probably toys, but they give us a good idea of what kind of carts the Indus people had and what their animals looked like.

The end of the civilisation

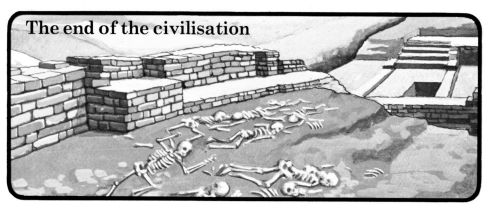

Excavations show that, by about 1700BC, Indus cities were less well-organized and poorer than before. The exact causes of this decline are not yet understood.

At Mohenjo-daro, remains have been found of bodies left unburied in the streets. This suggests the city was destroyed by enemies, possible invading Aryan people.

The Rise of Babylon

1

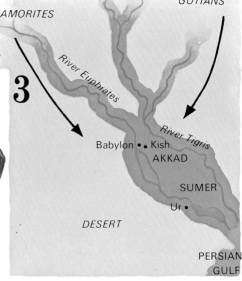

Bronze head of Sargon

About 2370BC, a new ruler appeared in Mesopotamia. His name was Sargon and he spoke a language called Akkadian. He conquered and united the city states of Mesopotamia for the first time.

2

One account of Sargon's life says he was found in a basket, floating on the river. He became cup-bearer to the king of the city of Kish, then overthrew him and took his place.

3

AMORITES

GUTIANS

River Euphrates

River Tigris

Babylon •• Kish

AKKAD

SUMER

Ur •

DESERT

PERSIAN GULF

Sargon built a capital city called Akkad, but its site has never been identified. His empire lasted 200 years and was then overthrown.

4

Gutian tribesmen invaded Mesopotamia, but later the rulers of the city of Ur gained control. Amorite invaders, however, were beginning to arrive.

5

Amorite families gained the rule of several cities. Babylon had an Amorite king called Hammurabi, who, in a series of brilliant wars, united Mesopotamia under his rule.

6

This monument shows Hammurabi being handed the symbols of justice by a god. Below is carved the law code he devised. It is the most complete law code known to us.

Hammurabi's laws

Some of Hammurabi's laws may seem harsh to us. For example, if a surgeon performed an operation that caused the death of a patient, his hand was cut off.

Another law said that if an architect built a house which collapsed and killed its owner, the architect was put to death.

Key dates

2371/2316 **Sargon** of Akkad.
2200 End of the Akkadian empire. Arrival of Gutian invaders.
2113 3rd Dynasty of Ur. Time when Ur ruled much of Mesopotamia.
2006 Overthrow of Ur. Cities of Isin and Larsa struggled for supremacy while Amorite invaders moved in.
1900 1st Dynasty of Babylon.
1792/1750 **Hammurabi** of Babylon.
1595 Babylon raided by Hittites From Anatolia, then taken over and ruled by tribesmen called Kassites.

Approximate BC dates

Myths

The people of Mesopotamia had many gods and goddesses. Here we have illustrated some of the stories they wrote about them.

Hammurabi made his god, Marduk, the most powerful god of Mesopotamia.

The priests told how Marduk had saved the world from the sea-monster Tiamat. The victory was celebrated each year at the New Year Festival.

The Mesopotamians thought the world was a flat disk. One story says that Marduk created the world by building a reed raft on the waters and pouring dust on it.

The great flood

Once, the gods were angry with men, and they decided to destroy them in a great flood. They warned one good man, Ut-napishtim, to build a boat.

The flood came and everything was destroyed except Ut-napishtim's boat, which came to rest on a mountain. He sent birds out, but they could find nowhere to settle.

Finally a raven was sent out and it did not return. The earth was beginning to dry out. Ut-napishtim and his family gave thanks to the gods for having been saved.

Gilgamesh

Gilgamesh was king of Uruk. His pride angered the gods and they made a half-beast, half-man called Enkidu to destroy him, but after fighting the two became friends.

They had many adventures but then Enkidu was killed. Afraid of death for the first time, Gilgamesh went to Ut-napishtim who had the secret of eternal life.

The secret was a plant which lived at the bottom of the sea. Gilgamesh dived and picked it, but on his way home it was eaten by a snake as he slept, so he did not live for ever.

These pictures are based on the style used by Sumerians and Babylonians on their cylinder seals.

Royal Graves of Anatolia

The people of Anatolia, which is the area now called Turkey, were among the world's first farmers. Later they acquired wealth through trading metal.

Anatolia was divided into several kingdoms, each with its own rulers. Rich royal graves have been found in some cities. They are dated between 2400BC and 2200BC.

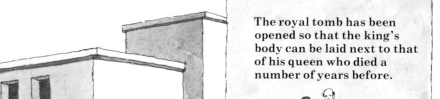

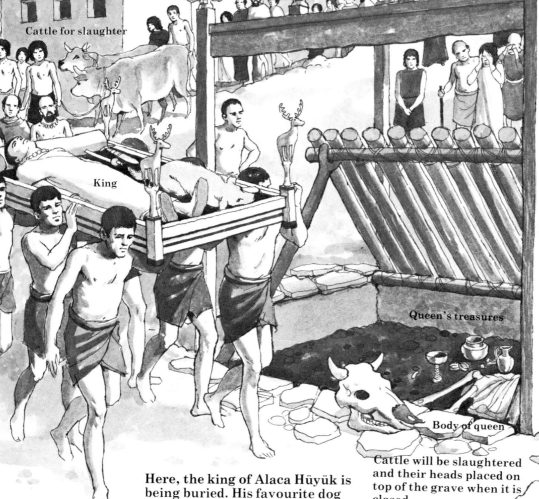

The royal tomb has been opened so that the king's body can be laid next to that of his queen who died a number of years before.

Cattle for slaughter

King

Queen's treasures

Body of queen

Cattle will be slaughtered and their heads placed on top of the grave when it is closed.

Here, the king of Alaca Hüyük is being buried. His favourite dog has been killed so that he can accompany his master on the last journey.

Troy · Dorak

Alaca Hüyük ·

ANATOLIA

Kültepe ·

MEDITERRANEAN SEA

The New Kingdom

The period archaeologists call the New Kingdom of Egypt began about 1567BC. Egypt was already an old civilisation with great achievements, but now a new age began. Great warrior kings like Tuthmosis III, Amenhotep II, Seti I and Ramesses II won a great empire. It was a time of great wealth, mighty temple buildings and religious conflicts. Only one king's tomb escaped being robbed in ancient times—that of Tutankhamun. His treasures give us an idea of the fabulous riches that must once have been in Egypt.

Queen Hatshepsut, who was one of the few women pharaohs of Egypt, inspects her new temple building at Deir el Bahari. With her is her architect Senenmut. The temple still stands today, though much of the paint has worn off.

Senenmut

Hatshepsut

This is part of Abu Simbel, a mighty rock-cut temple in Nubia which was built by Ramesses II.

The Egyptian Empire

By 1500BC, many countries in the Middle East already had long, interesting histories. Then, there was a great new burst of activity. Countries began to increase trade, win empires and set up colonies.

The Egyptians had lived peacefully since about 3120BC. The only province they had conquered in this time was Nubia, their neighbour in the south. Between 1670 and 1567BC, a people called the Hyksos crossed the eastern frontier and conquered Egypt.

The Egyptians built huge forts, like this one, on their frontiers. But the Hyksos had horses and chariots and they galloped past before the Egyptians could stop them.

The Hyksos ruled parts of Egypt for about 100 years before the Egyptians began to attack them. Most Egyptian soldiers still fought on foot, with spears or bows and arrows and no body armour.

The pharaoh's court

The pharaoh and his queen received ambassadors from lands belonging to their empire. These brought riches as gifts and tribute and also goods to trade. Here, Syrians and Nubians pay tribute to the pharaoh.

The Egyptians had their own gold mines and could use the gold to buy things they lacked, such as good timber. They also imported silver, copper, horses, slaves, ivory and exotic African animals and skins.

Lady courtiers

Gold

Syrians

Slave girl

Nubians

Pet baboon for the queen.

Ivory

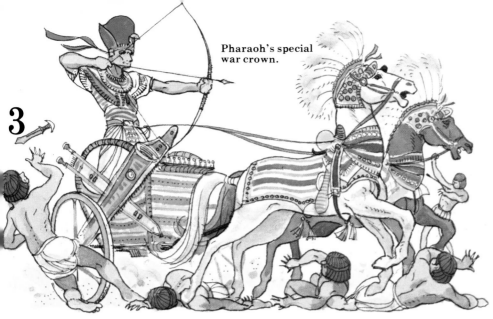

Pharaoh's special war crown.

3

4

The Egyptians had to learn to use horses and chariots to force the Hyksos out of Egypt. Then, led by warrior pharaohs (kings), they began to attack neighbouring lands.

Reports of the battles were written on temple walls to honour the pharaohs. Within 70 years, the Egyptians gained control of the largest empire of their time.

This map shows the Egyptian empire in 1450BC. The Mitanni and the Hittites in the north were powerful rivals of the Egyptians.

Trade with other lands

The Cretans, and later the Mycenaeans, traded with the Egyptians. They brought to Egypt the products of Crete, Greece and the Mediterranean islands.

The Egyptians visited a land they called Punt, which historians think may have been in east Africa. They bought incense there.

For centuries, Sinai was the source of Egypt's turquoise and copper. Donkey caravans regularly visited the mining camps to take supplies and bring the turquoise back.

Travel in ancient Egypt

Small boat for ferrying people across river.

Cargo boat taking goods to different parts of Egypt.

Boats travelling south used a sail to help against the flow of the current.

The easiest way to travel in Egypt was by river. Land travel was difficult because of the number of irrigation canals. Here are some of the boats which could be seen on the Nile about 3,000 years ago.

35

Houses and Furniture

This is a city street in ancient Egypt. Models show that in cities, where land was scarce, the Egyptians built houses up to five storeys high.

In Egypt, only temples and tombs, which were built to stand for ever, were made of stone. All other buildings were made of sun-dried bricks. Rich people had their houses plastered and painted.

Very few Egyptian cities can be excavated because modern cities are built on top of the old ones. However, models and paintings from tombs show us what ancient Egyptian houses looked like in both town and country.

Bedroom

Head-rest

The Egyptians used stone or wooden head-rests on their beds instead of pillows. They kept their clothes in chests and their jewellery and cosmetics in small boxes.

People spent a lot of time on the roofs of their houses because it was cooler there and they could enjoy the evening breeze. Sometimes they slept on the roof too.

Bathroom

Taking a shower

Lavatory

Rich people had bathrooms and lavatories in their houses. The bathroom walls were lined with stone to stop the splashes damaging the mud bricks.

1 Making bricks

The hard, dry earth was broken up with digging sticks and piled into baskets.

2

Water and chopped straw were trodden into the mud, and then the mixture was put into moulds.

3

The bricks were left to dry in the hot sun. It took several days for them to dry hard.

Furniture

The Egyptians buried furniture with the dead for use in the Next World, so archaeologists have been able to find many pieces of actual furniture. The greatest find of all was from the tomb of King Tutankhamun. The rich inlaid furniture shown here is of the type owned by noblemen. Some items are based on Tutankhamun's.

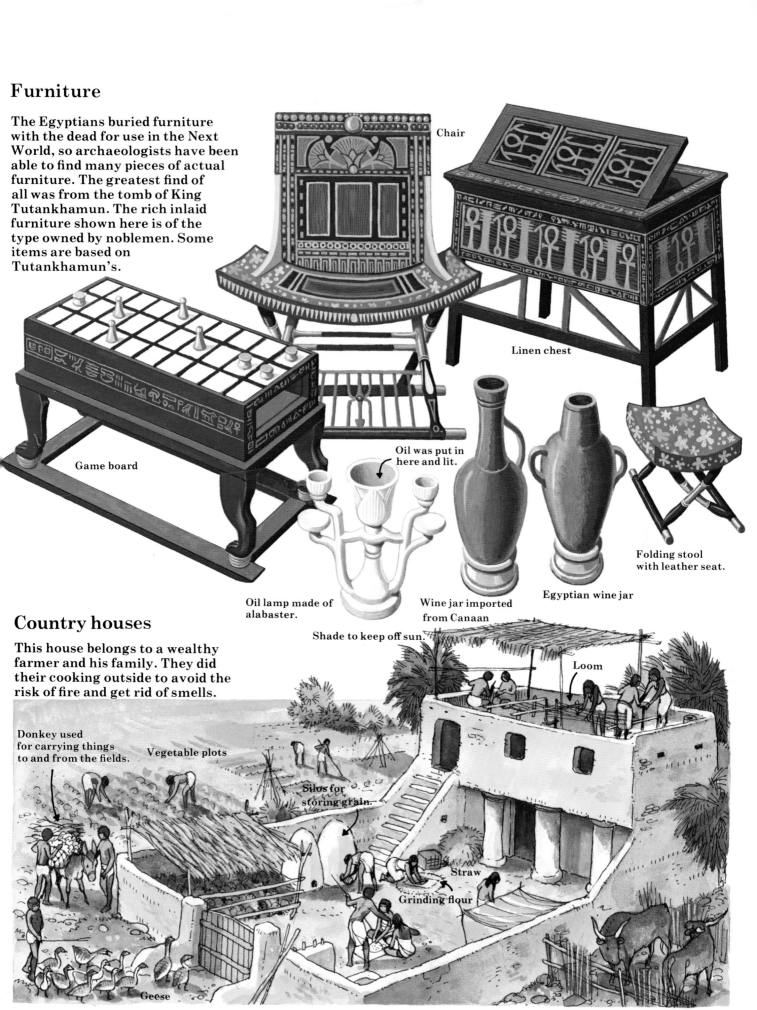

Chair

Linen chest

Game board

Oil was put in here and lit.

Folding stool with leather seat.

Oil lamp made of alabaster.

Wine jar imported from Canaan

Egyptian wine jar

Country houses

This house belongs to a wealthy farmer and his family. They did their cooking outside to avoid the risk of fire and get rid of smells.

Shade to keep off sun.

Loom

Donkey used for carrying things to and from the fields.

Vegetable plots

Silos for storing grain.

Straw

Grinding flour

Geese

Temples

1 The temple

Shrine

God

A statue of a god or goddess was kept in a special shrine in every Egyptian temple. Each day, priests bathed, clothed and "fed" the statue and then prayed to it.

2

Shrine

The main part of the temple was this huge columned hall. Its walls and pillars were covered with religious pictures and texts. Ordinary people were not allowed

in here or in the inner sanctuary where the shrine was kept. They had to stay outside in the temple courtyard. On festival days, they could see the shrine containing

1 Temple craftsmen

Egyptian temples owned large estates and were very rich. Many carpenters, leatherworkers, potters and other craftsmen were employed in the temple workshops.

2

Reed cut into strips.

Outside cut off

Papyrus reeds were gathered.

Strips soaked

Strips pounded

The Egyptians wrote on papyrus, which was made from papyrus reeds. These were cut into strips, soaked and then laid in two layers. Pounding with a mallet changed the layers into a solid sheet.

3

Blocks of ink

King's palette

Ordinary scribe's palette

Armies of scribes worked in the temples. Many of them spent their time copying out texts on rolls of papyrus. They wrote in picture signs, which we call hieroglyphs.

The scribes wrote on the papyrus with brushes. Their ink was made in solid blocks and had to be used with water. Brushes and inks were kept in palettes like these.

How we know

Only a few papyrus rolls have survived and these are badly damaged. However, scholars are able to learn a great deal from them about life in ancient Egypt.

Gods

the god. The priests lifted it on to a model boat which you can see here. Then they carried it around the city, accompanied by temple dancers and musicians.

Here are some of the Egyptians' gods and goddesses. They were often painted or carved in the shape of animals, or at least with animals'

heads. This was so that they could be easily recognised, even by people who could not read. Amen-Re was the chief of the gods.

Mathematics

The Egyptians were excellent mathematicians. Some of their texts show how they planned buildings and calculated the men and materials needed to build them.

Medicine

Surviving medical texts show the Egyptians were skilled doctors. These texts give details of treatments, medicines, prayers and spells.

Key dates

1570	**Ahmosis I** drove out the Hyksos. Beginning of empire.
1525/1512	**Tuthmosis I.** Warrior pharaoh who reached the River Euphrates on a raid. First King to have a rock-cut tomb in the Valley of the Kings at Thebes.
1503/1482	**Hatshepsut.** Queen who became pharaoh.
1504/1450	**Tuthmosis III.** Hatsheput's stepson. She kept him from power when he was young, but he later became the greatest of Egypt's warrior pharaohs.
1378/1362	**Akhenaten.** Pharaoh who tried to persuade Egyptians there was only one god. He was married to Nefertiti.
1361/1352	**Tutankhamun.** Boy pharaoh whose magnificent treasure was found by archaeologist Howard Carter in AD 1922.
1304/1237	**Ramesses II**, also called **Ramesses the Great**. Warrior pharaoh who fought the Hittites in the Battle of Kadesh.
1198/1166	**Ramesses III.** The last of Egypt's great warrior pharaohs. He saved Egypt from the Sea Peoples.
1166	After the death of Ramesses III, the power of Egypt slowly declined and the empire was lost.
751/671	Nubians ruled Egypt.
671/664	Assyrians ruled Egypt.
525/404	Persians ruled Egypt.
332	**Alexander the Great** conquered Egypt.

Approximate BC dates

Telling the time

Position of water level shows what time it is.

Water drips out of here.

This water clock was an Egyptian invention for telling the time. The Egyptians also worked out the 365 day calendar by studying the stars and planets.

Make a water clock

WATER

MARK WATER LEVEL WITH WAX CRAYON EACH MINUTE

BOWL

PIN-HOLE

YOGURT POTS

Fill up the top pot with water. Mark the water level with a wax crayon. Using a clock or watch, mark the water level each minute. Fill up the pot to use the clock.

Warriors of Anatolia

The Hittites were a tough warrior people. No-one is certain where they came from, but around 2000BC they arrived in Anatolia, which is in modern Turkey. The people they found there lived in rich cities each ruled by its own king. By 1680BC, the Hittites had defeated them all and ruled the whole land. About 200 years later, the Hittites began conquering the lands around them too, and building up an empire.

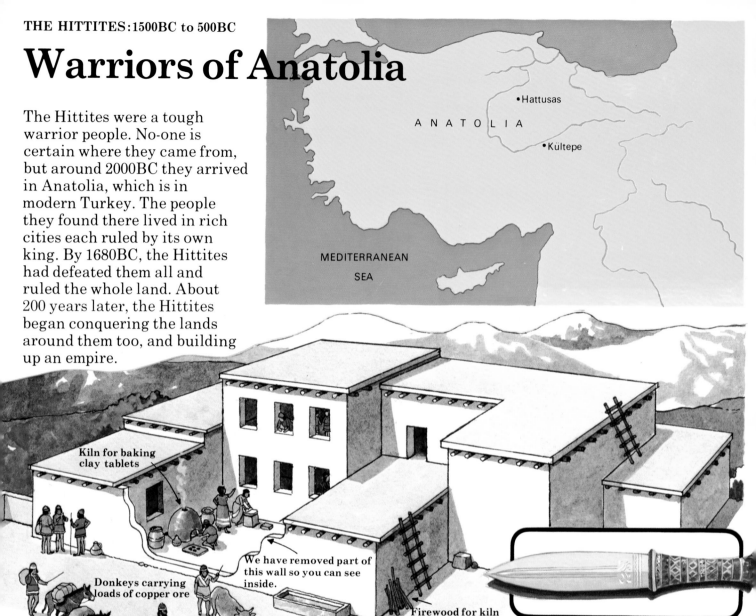

Kiln for baking clay tablets

We have removed part of this wall so you can see inside.

Donkeys carrying loads of copper ore

Firewood for kiln

Copper was found in Anatolia. Assyrian copper merchants built this trading post there about 2000BC.

The Hittites later forced out such foreign traders and took over the metal trade themselves. This made them very powerful because everyone needed metal for tools and weapons.

About 1500BC, the Hittites began trading iron which is much stronger than copper. This dagger, which belonged to Tutankhamun, has an iron blade which was probably a gift from the Hittites.

Key dates

2000	Hittites arrive in Anatolia.
1680/1650	**King Labarnas I** united the land.
1460	Beginning of Hittite empire.
1380/1340	**King Shuppiluliuma** extended empire into Syria and broke power of Mitanni.
1300	Battle of Kadesh against Ramesses II of Egypt.
1283	Peace treaty with Ramesses II.
1270	Hittite princess married Ramesses II.
1190	Hittites defeated by Sea Peoples. End of kingdom in Anatolia. Small states survive in Syria.
700	These states disappear in Assyrian empire.

Approximate BC dates

1 Hittite gods

Carvings are here.

This rocky gorge was very sacred to the Hittites. They carved pictures of their gods and goddesses into the rock-face there. In front are the ruins of a temple.

2

Teshub

This picture shows some of the gods and goddesses which are carved in the sacred gorge. The chief god was Teshub, who was thought to control the weather.

Hittite cities

The Hittites built massive defences with huge blocks of stone to guard their cities and palaces. This is part of the wall which surrounded their capital city, Hattusas.

Gateway to city

Hittite warriors

The Hittites dug narrow tunnels under their city walls. During a siege, they could dash out and surprise the enemy.

Secret passage

The Hittites' horses were too small to carry riders far. The warriors rode into battle in small chariots pulled by two or more horses.

Hittite warriors destroyed the Mitanni people and took their land. They also captured part of the Egyptians' empire.

Peace treaty

After years of war, the Hittites made peace with the Egyptians, and in 1270BC a Hittite princess married the Egyptian king Ramesses II. They also signed a treaty—the first international treaty for which we have the terms.

1 The end of the Hittites

Invading Sea Peoples

About 1200BC, the Hittite empire was wiped out by new invaders called the Sea Peoples, who probably came from the Mediterranean islands. They brought their familes with them to look for new homes.

2

Some Hittite refugees escaped to the south and settled in what is now Syria. They managed to survive there until the area was conquered by the Assyrians.

41

Mysterious People from Greece

The Mycenaeans are named after the city of Mycenae in Greece where their remains were first discovered in AD1876. Historians disagree about who they were, but some think they were new-comers to the area, related to the people who began arriving all over the Middle East around 2000BC.

This is the gold funeral mask of one of the first kings of Mycenae. It was once thought to be a portrait of Agamemnon, who led a famous war against Troy, but it is now known to be much earlier.

Mycenae was found by a German archaeologist called Schliemann. One of his greatest discoveries was this circle of royal graves dated between 1600 and 1500BC, early in Mycenaean history.

Tombs of the warrior kings

After 1500BC, the warrior kings of Mycenae and the other city-states in Greece were buried in tombs like this, called tholos tombs.

We have removed part of the mound of earth so you can see inside.

Doorway

The king's body, with his weapons and treasures, was placed in this bee-hive-shaped stone vault. The treasure was stolen from this tomb in ancient times and it was found empty.

This one, found at Mycenae, was called the Treasury of Atreus, because it was thought at first that it belonged to Agamemnon's father, Atreus.

The Mycenaean warrior kings became very rich and powerful and eventually rivalled the Cretans. When Crete was destroyed, they took control of the seas.

Key dates

2200/2000	New people arrived in Greece.
1600/1500	Grave circles at Mycenae. Mycenaeans influenced by Crete.
1450	Mycenaeans appear to have taken over Knossos in Crete. Linear B tablets in Crete as well as in Greece.
1400	Mycenaeans were great sea power. They traded widely.
1200	Siege of Troy. Slow decline of Mycenaean power.
1100/800	Dark Age in Greece.

Approximate BC dates

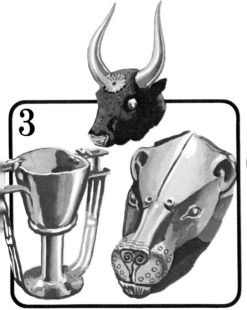

3

These are some of the objects found in the royal graves. Some of them, especially the bull's head, show that the Mycenaeans were influenced by the Cretans.

4

This tablet lists horses and chariots.

The Mycenaeans' language was an early form of Greek, and it was written in a script we call Linear B. Many tablets have been found but they are only lists of stored goods, showing that the wheat, barley, wine and olive oil produced by the local farmers were stored in the palace. They tell us nothing of the Mycenaeans' history or their thoughts.

5

This Mycenaean gold ring shows a goddess attended by her priestesses. As in Crete, goddesses and priestesses were very powerful, though tablets name some gods, too.

Mycenaean treasure

A balloon full of air is tied to the ingot to lift it to the surface.

"Ox-hide" ingot

Underwater archaeologists have rescued cargo from the wrecks of Mycenaean ships. The Mycenaeans sailed great distances to trade metals and other goods. They carried copper ingots shaped like stretched-out ox hides, like the one shown here.

How we know

The Mycenaeans traded valuable objects made by their craftsmen for things they needed from abroad. The presence of their special style of pottery, silver and gold work in other countries shows how far they travelled.

Silver bowl

Gold earrings

Pottery vase, with Mycenaean soldiers painted on it.

Perfume jar

Carved ivory of two women and a child, which shows us the clothes they wore.

Palaces and Soldiers

Mycenaean kings lived in great palaces. A porch and a reception room led into the megaron which was a central hall like this one, with a throne. The walls were covered with bright frescoes, which are pictures which were painted while the plaster was still damp.

These Mycenaean nobles were warriors, like their king.

There were many other rooms in the palace, including stores and record offices. Bedrooms were upstairs.

Bards sang songs in praise of the king.

Perfume jar

Step

Bath made of stone

Bronze helmet covered with boars' tusks.

Bronze armour

Shield covered with animal skin.

A bath like this was found in the palace at Pylos. Walled cities like Pylos, Mycenae and Athens had secret passages to underground springs, so they had water even during a siege.

We know a good deal about the armour and weapons of the Mycenaeans because weapons were found in their graves and pictures of soldiers have survived. It was probably only very noble or successful warriors who had complete suits of armour and boars' tusk helmets.

Hunting wild boars

Important warriors owned horses and chariots. When they were not at war they used them for hunting. The helmets they wore in battle were often decorated with tusks of wild boars killed in the hunt.

The Lion Gate

Many palaces and cities were protected by massive stone walls. This is the Lion Gate in the wall round Mycenae as it stands today.

The Trojan wars

The engraving on this piece of silver shows the siege of a city. A famous Greek story tells how the Mycenaeans sailed east to the city of Troy and laid siege to it for ten years.

Wars between the Mycenaean kingdoms may have weakened them, because about 1100BC new people called the Dorians invaded some areas of Greece. The power of the Mycenaeans declined, though their glory lived on in the poems of the Greek poet Homer.

Rich Mycenaean ladies wore dresses like this. Helen of Troy, a beautiful lady who was supposed to have been the cause of the wars with Troy, would have dressed like this too.

Canaanites and Philistines

The people who settled at the the eastern end of the Mediterranean about 2000BC are called the Canaanites. Their land was rich and it also formed an important link between Asia and Africa. Rival empire builders such as the Egyptians, Mitanni and Hittites constantly fought over it.

By 1500BC there were many walled city-states in Canaan. They were heavily defended and each had its own royal family and palace. This statue is of one of the Canaanite princes.

Victorious warrior
Queen congratulating prince
Prisoners

This piece of ivory shows a Canaanite prince being welcomed home after a battle. The princes were always fighting each other instead of working together to keep out invaders.

Huge cedar trees grew in part of Canaan. The people of Egypt and Mesopotamia wanted these because they had no good wood of their own. This made them anxious to gain control of the area.

The port of Byblos

Slaves

Merchant

Scribe

Engraved gold trays

Wine jars

Cedar wood

Canaanite craftsmen were very skilled. They made beautiful objects from gold and ivory which were sold to other countries. Here, a Canaanite merchant

is preparing to set out from the great port of Byblos about 1450BC. He is going to take slaves, wood, wine, gold and ivory to his best customers, the Egyptians.

Canaanite gods

Canaanite
script

Clay tablets, like this, were found in the remains of the city of Ugarit. They are covered with Canaanite writing which tells of the adventures of gods and goddesses.

Two of the gods are shown here. The Canaanites believed their gods controlled the weather and made the crops grow. They worshipped them in "High Places" which had tall stones inside.

The Sea Peoples invade

About 1190BC, the Sea Peoples invaded the eastern Mediterranean, killing and destroying as they went. Here they are fighting the Egyptians, who finally defeated them.

One tribe of Sea Peoples, the Peleset, retreated to the south of Canaan and settled there. This land was named Palestine after them and in the Bible they are called Philistines.

Egyptians

Philistines

The Philistines took control of the local iron trade. Iron weapons are much stronger than copper and bronze, so the Philistines were powerful and feared.

Nomads in the Desert

Even in our earliest records there are references to tribes who wandered along the edges of the Syrian and Arabian deserts with their sheep. Such people are called nomads.

This is part of an Egyptian tomb painting of about 1900BC. It shows the arrival of nomad traders who have brought eye-paint to sell in Egypt. They carry their trade goods and all their belongings on the backs of donkeys. Other tribes owned sheep and goats which they took into the Delta of Egypt to eat the grass.

In some places nomads were able to settle among the farmers, but if too many arrived the locals drove them away.

This statue is of a king whose tribe had invaded and become the rulers of the city of Mari in Mesopotamia. He lived about 2000BC.

Solomon's temple

This temple was built in Jerusalem by the Israelite king, Solomon. Solomon and his father, David, were friendly with the Phoenician king, Hiram, of Tyre. Hiram sent skilled Phoenician craftsmen to Jerusalem to help design and build the temple. It is very similar in plan to earlier temples built by the Canaanites.

Cedar wood beams

Holy of Holies

Wood carvings covered with gold leaf

Altar

Some nomads, like this girl musician, hired themselves out as servants. Others became paid soldiers or labourers.

By about 1000BC, people had learnt to tame camels. This meant they could cross the desert.

The Israelites

1. Among the wandering tribes were the ancestors of the Israelites. After many battles they took some land from the Canaanites and settled down.

2. The Philistines were serious rivals. The Israelites chose Saul as king to lead them against the Philistines, but the hero of the war is said to have been a boy called David.

Solomon's temple

3. David became king in about 1010BC and made Jerusalem his capital. This great bronze bowl stood outside the temple built there by his son Solomon.

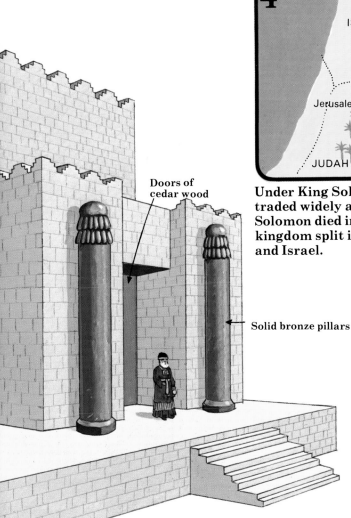

Doors of cedar wood

Solid bronze pillars

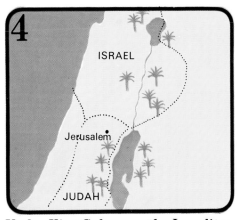

4. Under King Solomon, the Israelites traded widely and grew rich. After Solomon died in 925BC, the kingdom split in two—Judah and Israel.

5. Gradually the Assyrians extended their empire towards Israel. This monument shows King Jehu of Israel paying tribute to them. Later, Israel rebelled and its people were taken away, never to return.

6. The people of Judah escaped the Assyrians, but were conquered and taken into captivity by the Babylonians in 587BC. Jerusalem and the temple were destroyed.

Many of these people and places are mentioned in the Old Testament.

49

The Phoenicians

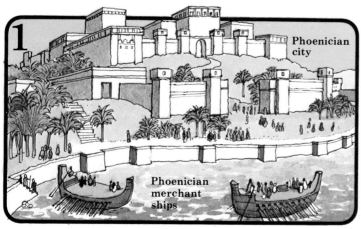

About 1100BC, trade in the Mediterranean was dominated by rich Canaanite merchants who lived on the coast. The Greeks gave them the name Phoenicians. Phoenician cities had splendid harbours and strong defences. The greatest of them were Tyre and Sidon.

Among the things the Phoenicians made and traded were brightly coloured glass vases and beads. Their most famous product was an expensive dye made from murex shells, which dyed cloth a range of beautiful colours from pink to deep purple.

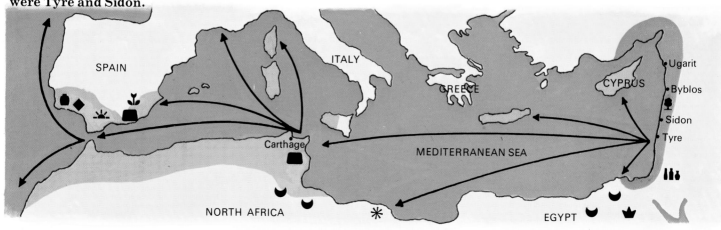

Phoenicia	ivory	lead	wood
	silver	olive oil	grain
Phoenician colonies	gold	salt	glass
	copper		

This map shows where the Phoenicians travelled and traded. Besides trading they also set up many colonies in foreign lands. The most important of these was Carthage in north Africa. Eventually these activities brought them into conflict with the Greeks and later the Romans.

Carthage

The founder of Carthage was the Phoenician princess Dido. When she landed on the coast of north Africa, she asked the local ruler for land on which to build a city.

He said she could have as much land as an ox-hide would cover. Dido had the hide cut into very thin strips so she could mark off a large area of land.

Occasionally in times of great trouble, the Phoenicians sacrificed children to their gods. The burnt remains were placed in pottery urns, like these, and buried.

3

The Phoenicians were on good terms with their Israelite neighbours. Ahab, king of Israel, married Jezebel, princess of Tyre, and Phoenician craftsmen helped build Solomon's temple.

War ships

The Phoenicians were famous for their war ships. This one is a bireme, which means it has two banks of oars.

4

The Phoenicians were skilled sailors and daring explorers. One expedition visited the west coast of Africa and another sailed right round it.

Phoenicia

AFRICA

5

Part of the Phoenician alphabet.

Letters in our alphabet which have come from the Phoenician ones.

Perhaps the greatest of all the Phoenicians' achievements was the invention of their alphabet, which is the basis of the alphabet we use today.

Key dates

1100	Rise to power of Phoenicians.
970/936	**Hiram the Great**, king of Tyre.
876	Tyre paid tribute to Assyria.
875	**Jezebel** married Ahab of Israel.
814	**Dido** founded Carthage.
600	Phoenicians sailed round Africa.
574	Tyre defeated by Babylon.
539	Phoenicia became part of Persian empire with fall of Babylon.
	Approximate BC dates

Ram for making holes in enemy ships.

Later, Phoenicia became part of the Persian empire. The Persians used Phoenician war ships to fight great sea battles against the Greeks.

Life in the Assyrian Empire

In early times, Assyria was a small, unimportant state in northern Mesopotamia. For centuries it was ruled by more powerful states, such as Akkad and Babylon. When these collapsed, the Assyrians had the chance to become independent and win an empire of their own.

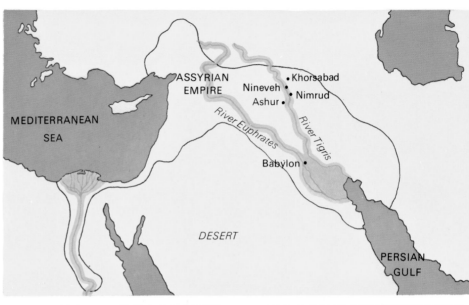

This carving shows one of the Assyrians' many gods. Their chief god was Ashur. They also worshipped a great mother goddess, Ishtar, and believed in demons and spirits.

This is the capital city of Assyria, which was named Ashur after the god. It was built on the River Tigris so that trading ships could unload there.

Ashur had a powerful Council of Elders. It was often in conflict with the king and many kings tried to reduce its power.

The Assyrians, like the Babylonians, had a code of laws. People who broke them were punished savagely. Some were flogged or had their ears cut off.

This is an Assyrian library. The language and literature inherited from Sumer and Babylon were stored on clay tablets.

The Assyrians dug deep wells inside their cities. If the city were besieged, the people would still have water.

52

The empire

1 For centuries, the Assyrian peasants had to fight for survival. They became good, tough warriors.

2 This is Ashurnasirpal II. His grandfather, Adadnirari II, had made Assyria independent. He made it into an empire.

3 By 670BC the empire was too big to be controlled properly. First Egypt, then Babylon, broke away.

4 By 609BC the empire was destroyed. Its ruins lay forgotten in the desert until they were discovered in the 1840s.

Watering the land

This is a shaduf. The Assyrians used shadufs to lift river water into canals dug specially to take it to the fields.

Stone weight

When the land was watered properly, it was fertile. The Assyrians grew wheat, barley, grapes, fruit trees and vegetables.

This aqueduct was built to take water to Nineveh so that King Sennacherib could have gardens and orchards planted there.

How to make a model shaduf

Use this model shaduf to lift water from a bowl into another.

SCISSORS
TAPE
3
BOTTLE TOP
HOLE

1
BAG
TIE ON STRING

2

PAPER CLIP
4
TOP
PLASTICINE WEIGHT

STICK

5
BOTTLE

YOU WILL NEED:
STRING
STICKY TAPE
A STICK (30 CM LONG)
PAPER CLIP
BOTTLE WITH SCREW TOP
PLASTICINE
CORNER CUT OFF PLASTIC BAG

The weight at the end of the pole balanced the bucket when it was full. The farmer then swung the pole around and emptied the bucket into the canal.

Leather bucket

Kings and their Palaces

The palaces were decorated inside with glazed tiles and stone carvings showing the king's great deeds.

The Assyrians believed that their land belonged to the god Ashur. The king, as Ashur's servant, ruled the land, waged war in his name, built temples and appointed priests and led important religious festivals.

Assyrian kings usually had many wives and children. The son chosen by the king to be his heir was specially educated in the "House of the Succession" to be a good ruler.

This is King Ashurnasirpal II in the throne room of his palace. Here, the king receives royal messengers from all parts of the empire who keep him in touch with what is happening.

Ashurnasirpal and several other kings fought hard to enlarge the empire. To celebrate, they used prisoners of war to build their splendid palaces and cities in Khorsabad, Nineveh and Nimrud.

King's personal servant

Servant carrying the king's weapons.

The palace garden

King Ashurbanipal relaxes in his garden with the queen and his servants and musicians.

His garden is planted with exotic trees and flowers gathered from all over the empire.

Musicians

Lion hunting

When not leading the army in war, the king hunted to show his skill and bravery. Lions were brought specially to his hunting parks.

Walls of soldiers with their shields stop the lions escaping.

Lions were kept in cages until the king was ready for them.

King Ashurbanipal

Grape vines

Servants with fans

Queen

King

Furniture decorated with gold and ivory inlays.

The Assyrian Army

1 Going into battle

The Assyrians had to fight continually to keep their empire under control. Here the army is setting out to attack a city which has rebelled against their rule.

The foot soldiers were armed with bows and arrows, slings for hurling stones, or lances. The cavalry, that is the soldiers on horseback, also used bows and lances.

Horse-drawn chariots each carried a team of driver, bowman and shield-bearer. The army also had siege engines which had battering rams and space inside for bowmen.

Sacking the captured city

Often, the Assyrians completely destroyed the captured city and the farmland around it. They took its treasure as booty and either killed the citizens or took them captive.

Houses in the city have been set on fire.

Soldiers knock down the city walls.

Orchards are burnt.

Valuable goods and animals are taken away as booty.

Heads of dead citizens are collected and counted.

Captives are led away.

Some of the captives became slaves, but others were sent to live in new cities. The Assyrians hoped that their experiences would teach them not to rebel again.

The soldiers swam across rivers clutching inflated animal skins to help them keep afloat. The horses swam too. The chariots were rowed across in small round boats.

Inside a siege engine

The siege engines were made of wood and covered with animal's skins. They could be pushed up to the city walls with several bowmen hidden inside. The ram was used for breaking down gates and undermining walls.

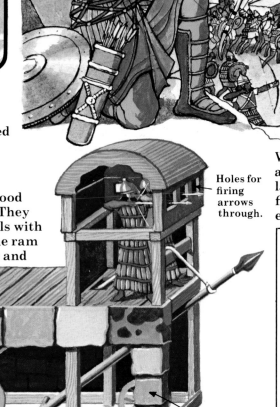

Holes for firing arrows through.

The engine was moved by soldiers pushing from behind.

The battering ram was raised and lowered by this rope.

Wooden frame

Animal skins

When they reached the city, heavily armed soldiers scaled the walls with ladders while bowmen and slingers fired from further away. Siege engines battered the wall and gate.

Key dates

2000	**Pazur-Ashur I** reigned about the time Assyria became independent of Sumerian empire.	
1814/1782	**Shamsi-Adad I.** First king to extend Assyria's frontiers.	
911/891	**Adad-nirari II** united his people.	
883/859	**Ashurnasirpal II**	
858/824	**Shalmaneser III**	
721/705	**Sargon II**	
704/681	**Sennacherib**	
668/631	**Ashurbanipal**	
614/609	Complete destruction of empire.	

Approximate BC dates

The conquered people

Local prince

Assyrian official

Conspirators planning rebellion

Some conquered lands, such as Egypt, were ruled by local princes, but Assyrian officials stayed to make sure they were loyal. Even so, as the empire grew, rebellions were common.

Assyrian scribe

People bringing tribute

Conquered people had to pay tribute to the Assyrians. Failure to do so was rapidly punished and the Assyrians were notorious for the cruel tortures they inflicted on people.

The City of Babylon

The ancient city of Babylon stood on the banks of the River Euphrates. Under its great king, Hammurabi, Babylon controlled an empire, but this gradually broke up after he died about 1750BC.

For several hundred years Babylon was ruled peacefully by a people called the Kassites. In 1171BC, the Kassites were driven out by the Elamites. A troubled time followed. The Assyrians then claimed to rule Babylon, but some Babylonians resisted them.

The marshes of southern Mesopotamia made a good hiding place for Babylonians fighting against Assyrian rule. One of their leaders was Merodach-Baladan.

With the help of their neighbours, the Medes, the Babylonians defeated the Assyrians in 612BC. Nebuchadnezzar, the son of their general, went on to win an empire.

Telling the future

The Babylonians believed they could tell the future by looking at a sheep's liver. This clay model was made as a guide to the different parts for the priests to look at.

Key dates

1500/1350	The Kassites ruled in peace. After 1350 there were wars with the Elamites and Assyrians.
1171	Kassite rule ended by Elamites.
729	**Tiglathpileser** of Assyria became king of Babylon.
721/711	**Merodach-Baladan** led resistance to Assyria.
689	**Sennacherib** of Assyria destroyed Babylon.
626/605	**Nabopolassar** led fight against Assyrians, with help of Medes.
605/562	**Nebuchadnezzar** ruled Babylon.
556/539	**Nabonidus** ruled Babylon.
539	Babylon captured by Persians.

Approximate BC dates

Ishtar Gate

Processional Way

Part of the New Year procession

Courtyard houses

This huge ziggurat and temple, which Nebuchadnezzar built, was dedicated to the Babylonians' chief god, Marduk.

The city of Babylon was rebuilt by Nebuchadnezzar and it became one of the richest cities in the world. The city was entered through a huge gateway, covered with glazed blue tiles, called the Ishtar Gate. Nearby was Nebuchadnezzar's magnificent palace, with its famous Hanging Garden.

Nebuchadnezzar's palace

Water from the river was used to water the Hanging Gardens.

These are the Hanging Gardens of Babylon. They were built by Nebuchadnezzar for his wife Amytis, a princess of the Medes, because she missed the hilly landscape of her home.

Processional Way

The people of Babylon are watching a procession make its way to the temple of Marduk for the New Year festival. Old traditions like this were revived when Babylon was rebuilt.

City walls

The goddess Ishtar

This is a statue of Ishtar, the chief goddess of Babylon after whom the great gate was named. It is carved from alabaster and has rubies inlaid in it.

The end of Babylon

Royal Persian Guardsmen

In 539BC, Babylon was taken over by the Persians whose power was rapidly increasing. People gradually left the city and by AD200, it was deserted and ruined.

Monument Builders

The climate of North Europe is so damp that things buried in the ground decay quickly and leave little trace for archaeologists. Because of this we know less about the people of Europe than about the people of the Middle East. No texts have been found, so we do not know if they could write. From very early times, however, people in Europe built great stone monuments, and the treasures that have survived show they were highly skilled craftsmen.

After about 600BC, some Celts spread out across Europe in these directions.

Treasures of Europe

These are just a few examples of the fine craftsmanship of the people living in Europe in ancient times.

Rock carvings like this were found in Sweden and Norway. They often show ships carrying the sun across the sky.

This bronze helmet is from Vixo in Denmark. It was probably not worn in battle because it is too heavy and awkward.

This is a bronze model of a chariot carrying the sun. It was thrown into a marsh in Denmark as an offering to the gods.

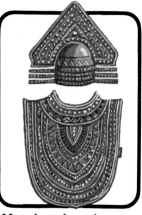

Metalworkers in Europe were very skilled. This helmet and armour came from Villanova in Italy.

This enormous bronze wine jar was made in Greece and then taken to France. It was buried in the grave of a princess.

Building Stonehenge

The most impressive of the ancient stone circles is Stonehenge in southern England. Work began on it about 2750BC. It was changed several times and here the last and most impressive version is being built. It was finished soon after 1500BC.

Stone pounders make hollows in lintels.

About a thousand men are needed to pull one of the sarsen stones from the **quarry over 32km away.**

This is Stonehenge when it was completed. It was probably a temple but some scholars think it was also used as a calendar.

Lintel

Blue-stones

Sarsen

Wooden rollers are placed under the sledge to make it move more easily.

These "bluestones" were brought from Wales and were used in an earlier stone circle. When this circle is finished, they will be put in the middle of it.

Sarsen being raised into position in its hole.

Sledge

These lumps fit in hollows on lintels.

The upright stones are called sarsens.

Tree-trunk lever

The chalky earth is taken away in baskets.

Pick made of antler.

These men are digging a hole for the next sarsen.

The lintels are lifted up on towers of logs placed criss-cross. The layers of logs are slipped under the stone one at a time to gradually raise the lintel to the top of the sarsens.

61

First Civilisation in China

Civilisation in China began near the Yellow River. Here, the Shang kings ruled for about 500 years, until a war-like people called the Chou conquered them in 1057BC.

The first farmers of northern China grew millet and kept cattle and pigs. They probably lived in pit houses dug out of the ground.

The kings lived in palaces built of wood and earth.

Pit houses with thatched roofs.

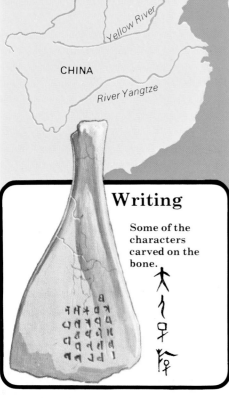

Writing

Some of the characters carved on the bone.

The earliest form of Chinese writing is found cut into animal bones. These were used for taking messages which were thought to come from the gods.

A Chou noble drives away from the king's palace in his war chariot. The chariot had no seat, just a platform to stand on.

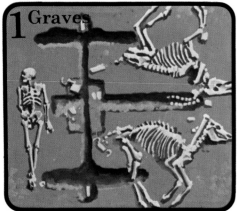

1 Graves

Recently the Chinese opened the tombs of the Shang kings near Anyang. They found the skeletons of horses and charioteers with their chariots.

2

The Shang king thought his ancestors were gods. He offered them meat and wine in bronze vessels like this one. Many Chinese still honour their ancestors today.

3

Jade ornaments like this animal were sewn to the dead person's clothes. Objects like this ornamental dagger were put in the graves of nobles and rich people.

First Farmers in America

Many different tribes lived in Central and Southern America. It seems that they became farmers later than the people in the Middle East.

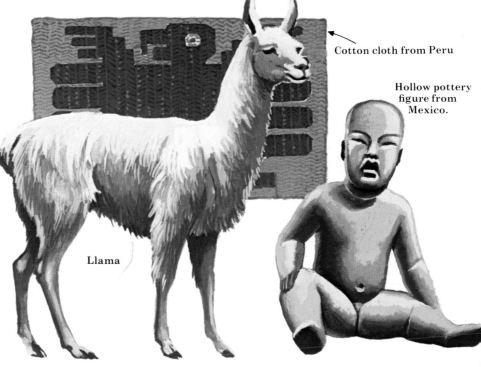

Cotton cloth from Peru

Llama

Hollow pottery figure from Mexico.

The farmers had been growing cotton since 3000BC. They spun and wove it by hand to make cloth with special designs like the one here. They got wool from llamas and alpacas.

Their most important crop was maize, which first appeared in Mexico in 2500BC. Pottery, like this figure was being made from 2300BC onwards.

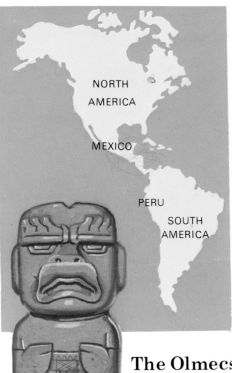

Olmec carving made of jade.

The Olmecs

The Olmecs, first of the famous cultures of this area, appear about 1200BC. You can recognize their statues and jade and pottery figures by their "baby" faces.

In Mexico, the Olmecs were building shrines on great mounds like this by 600BC. At this time they had no wheels or metal tools, so the buildings were an amazing achievement.

India

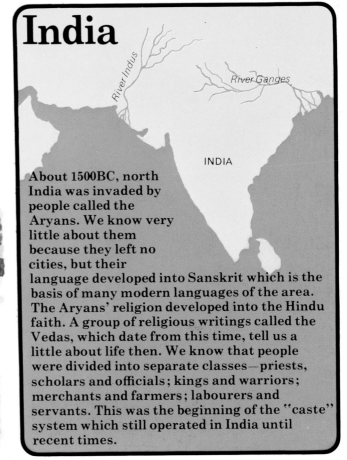

River Indus

River Ganges

INDIA

About 1500BC, north India was invaded by people called the Aryans. We know very little about them because they left no cities, but their language developed into Sanskrit which is the basis of many modern languages of the area. The Aryans' religion developed into the Hindu faith. A group of religious writings called the Vedas, which date from this time, tell us a little about life then. We know that people were divided into separate classes—priests, scholars and officials; kings and warriors; merchants and farmers; labourers and servants. This was the beginning of the "caste" system which still operated in India until recent times.

The Dark Ages

The years 1100 to 700BC in Greece are called the Dark Ages as so little is known about them. New people called the Dorians invaded and after that no more great palaces were built. People lived simply. They burnt their dead instead of burying them with offerings.

.It was now easier to get iron, so people could make strong tools and weapons. Greece was divided into several city-states, such as Corinth, Athens and Sparta, which often quarrelled amongst themselves.

1

This is Homer, who composed poems about the siege of Troy and the adventures of a hero called Odysseus. His poems were passed on by word of mouth for years until writing came into use again.

2

Greek letters

ABEKMNRT

ABEKMNRT

Our letters

The Greeks took over the Phoenician alphabet and adapted it to suit their own needs. It was so simple to use that many people could learn to read and write.

As the numbers of people grew, many went abroad. Some set up colonies in other countries and traded. Others hired themselves out to foreign kings as soldiers.

4

The Greeks were the first people to make coins of a standard weight and quality of metal. These made trade much easier and the traders became very rich.

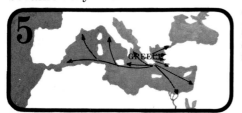

5

By trading and setting up colonies around the Mediterranean, the Greeks grew prosperous. They became dangerous competitors for the Phoenician merchants.

Soldiers

These are Greek soldiers called Hoplites. They fought in closely packed ranks, each man protecting the one next to him with his shield.

Iron spears

Bronze greaves to protect legs

In the cities, people rebelled against the unjust ruling nobles. With their help, new leaders seized power. These were called "tyrants".

Conquerors

The land we now call Iran was invaded by new people about 1200BC. The invaders seem to have come from somewhere in Europe, like many others who arrived in the Middle East from 2000BC onwards.

One Iranian tribe, called the Medes, became powerful and in 612BC helped to destroy the empire of the Assyrians. Another group was the Persians, who later took over the Babylonian empire. Led by a great king called Cyrus, the Persians then won a huge empire of their own.

Persepolis

King Darius, a successor of Cyrus began building an enormous palace at Persepolis in 518BC. The great hall, shown here, was big enough to hold 10,000 people.

African   Indus Valley people   Ionian   Scythian

Armenian   Babylonian   Median   Elamite

Parthian   Assyrian

The palace of Persepolis was burned down in 330BC by Alexander the Great, but some of the carvings survived. These pictures are of carvings on one of the great staircases which show some of the people conquered by the Persians. They are bringing horses, camels, skins, cloth and gold as tribute to the Persian king.

Great Hall

Persians   Medes

Visitors were led through many halls and terraces which were decorated with stone carvings. The palace does not seem to have been lived in by the kings. It was probably used for special ceremonies like the celebration of the New Year.

Here, important Persians and Medes wait to be received by the king.

65

The Persian Empire

The great Persian king, Darius I, ran his empire cleverly and efficiently. He collected taxes from all the conquered people, but allowed them to keep their own customs, religions and way of life as long as they were obedient. Darius appointed local governors, called satraps, to rule the provinces of the empire and used Persian soldiers to check that the satraps did not become too powerful. He also had good roads built so that messengers could travel quickly with news from all over the empire.

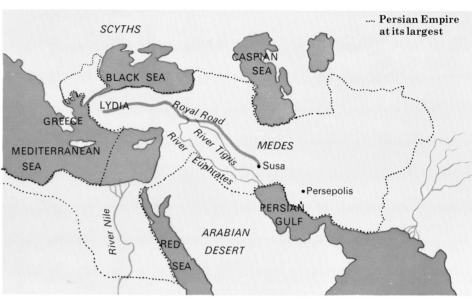

.... Persian Empire at its largest

1 The Crown Prince, Xerxes

Visitors must not go past this point.

King Darius I

Incense burners

The Persians lived in the land we now call Iran. They won a huge empire under their great king, Cyrus, whose successor, King Darius I, is shown here.

Darius organised the empire very efficiently. He appointed local governors, called satraps, to rule each province and used Persian soldiers to check that they did not become too powerful. He also had good roads built so that messengers could travel quickly with news from all over the empire.

2

As long as conquered people paid their taxes, the Persians treated them and their customs with respect. Here, officials check tax payments before storing them in the palace.

Religion

Fire was sacred to the Persians and the Magi (priests) kept one burning on an altar. A prophet, Zarathushtra, changed Persian religion from the worship of many gods to that of one, Ahuramazda.

Key dates

2000/1800	The Aryans migrated from southern Russia
628	Birth of **Zarathushtra** religious prophet.
559/529	Reign of **Cyrus the Great.**
547	**Cyrus** defeated King Croesus of Lydia.
521/486	Reign of **Darius I.**
513/512	First Asian invasion of Europe. Persians conquered Thrace and Macedon.
490	Persians defeated by Greeks at Battle of Marathon.
486/465	Reign of **Xerxes I**, son of Darius.
480	Persians defeated by Greeks at Salamis.
330	**Alexander** destroyed Persian Empire. Persepolis was burned.

Approximate BC dates

The Greeks at War

Until 1100BC, the Mycenaeans ruled Greece. Then the Dorians invaded and a troubled time followed when wealth and culture declined. We call this the Greek Dark Ages. Later prosperity gradually returned.

Meanwhile, the Persian empire was growing rapidly. The Persians conquered Lydia, until then a Greek area ruled by King Croesus, and forced the Greek cities there to pay "tribute" (a kind of tax) to them. Later, several of these cities, led by Athens, rebelled and the so-called "Persian Wars" began.

The Persian king, Darius I, invaded Greece, but was defeated at Marathon in 490BC. The news was carried over 40km to Athens by a runner. Our Olympic marathon race is named after this.

War with Greece was continued by Darius' son Xerxes. He built a bridge of boats to get his army across the Hellespont, using ropes and ships made by his Egyptian and Phoenician subjects.

The Athenians discovered a rich vein of silver in their mines and so had money to build a new fleet. They finally defeated the Persians in a battle off the coast of Salamis.

Athens became the greatest city of Greece. It led a league of Greek cities which were afraid that the Persians might attack again, and collected money from them.

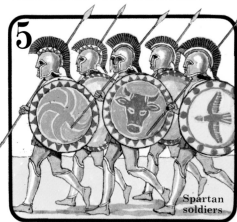

Athens' great leader Pericles built these fine new buildings to replace those damaged in the Persian wars. The other cities were angry because he used money belonging to the league to build them.

The state of Sparta led the enemies of Athens in a long and terrible war, known as the Peloponnesian War. It lasted 27 years until Athens was defeated in 404BC.

Life in Athens

Town life almost disappeared in Greece during the Dark Ages, but as trade slowly increased, the cities grew again. A city and the land around it formed a city-state. The largest and most famous of these was Athens. It had a high place, called the Acropolis, where the people could go in times of danger. All the "citizens", that is all the free men, not women or slaves, took part in the running of the city by voting on important matters. This is called democracy and it was first used in Athens.

The Parthenon temple, built by Pericles for the goddess Athena.

The old city, called the Acropolis.

The Sacred Way which leads to the Acropolis.

The Agora where people met to argue about politics and buy and sell things.

Open-air restaurant

Grape vines

Pottery high-ch[...]

Trade with Athens

Piraeus, the port of Athens, is about six kilometres away. Goods from all over the Mediterranean were landed there, including wine from the Aegean islands and grain from the Black Sea ports.

Theatre

Stage

Actors

Chorus

Altar

Orchestra

Padded actor from wall painting

Pottery copy of actor's mask

A Greek theatre had a round area called the orchestra where the actors performed. The audience often brought cushions to sit on because the seats were stone.

The idea of the theatre grew from dances held at festivals in honour of the gods. Later, writers like Euripedes and Sophocles produced plays specially for the theatre.

All the parts in plays were taken by men who wore masks and padding. Copies of the masks were made in pottery to decorate buildings

Politics

1 All "citizens" discussed and voted on city matters. Our word "politics" comes from the Greek *politikos*, which means "of the city".

Discs meaning "guilty"

Disc meaning "not guilty"

2 There were no lawyers, so people had to present their own cases in court. Jurors showed their verdicts with small discs like these.

PEDIKLES XSANΘIPPO

Ostraka

KIMON MILTIADES

Politician's name

ADISTEIDES ADIΦDONOS

3 A politician could be sent into exile if 6,000 citizens wrote his name on pieces of broken pottery like these, called ostraka.

4 The philosopher Socrates was condemned because some people feared the way he questioned everything. He chose to die and drank poison.

Potters' workshop

Potters' quarter of city

Pottery

Athens was famous for its pottery. Everyday things, like this baby's bottle and toy, were made of pottery, as well as fine vases painted with scenes of gods and heroes or daily life.

How we know

The scenes painted on vases tell us a lot about Greek life. This one shows a boy buying new sandals. He places his foot on the leather and the shoemaker cuts round it.

These women are celebrating the festival of the god Dionysus with wild dances. Most of the time women stayed at home and did not take part in public life.

Boys were well educated from the age of seven. This boy is learning to read. Music and sports were also taught. Girls stayed at home and were taught by their mothers.

Alexander the Great

The Greek city-states still quarrelled among themselves even when the Peloponnesian War was over. Peace was not restored until Philip, King of Macedon took control. The Greeks thought him a barbarian, which to them was anyone who was not Greek. Philip wanted to fight the Persians with Greek help, but he died leaving his son, Alexander, to carry out his plan. Alexander set out to conquer an empire.

Alexander was educated in the Greek way by the philosopher Aristotle. Like all Macedonians, though, he was a tough soldier.

Alexander crossed into Asia with his army and defeated the Persian king Darius III at the battle of Issus in 333BC. This Roman mosaic is a copy of a Greek painting showing Alexander at Issus.

He moved on through the Persian empire to Syria. The Phoenician city of Tyre was attacked with catapults on boats.

Egypt was easily conquered. Here, at the oasis of Siwa, Alexander was hailed as the son of the god Ammon. Some Greeks disapproved of this.

Alexander fought Darius again and finally defeated him in 331BC. Then he led his army through difficult mountainous country to Persepolis.

The Persian king's treasure was stored at Persepolis. Alexander's army captured and looted it and then set off towards India.

When they arrived in India, they won many battles, including one against King Porus, in which they met war elephants for the first time.

Alexander died of a fever in 323BC on the long trek home from India. His body was taken to Alexandria in Egypt and buried there.

Alexandria

Alexander founded many cities, all called Alexandria after him. The greatest of all was on the Mediterranean coast of Egypt. It became one of the most splendid cities of the ancient world. Alexander's general, Ptolemy, became King of Egypt and founded the Mouseion, a place where scholars could meet, talk and do scientific experiments. There was also a magnificent library containing many valuable books. Ptolemy's family ruled Egypt for 300 years.

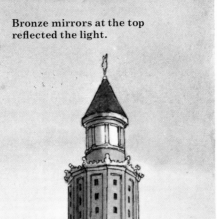
Bronze mirrors at the top reflected the light.

The Pharos

Many buildings were of Greek design with columns and statues.

Some Egyptian monuments, like this obelisk, were also erected.

The lighthouse of Alexandria, the Pharos, was one of the wonders of the world. Alexandrian merchants sailed to India and the East, bringing back spices and silks for sale in the Mediterranean world.

Science and inventions

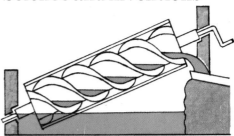

Many things were invented in Alexandria. Archimedes is said to have designed this screw, which lifts water from one level to another. It is still used today.

An astronomer called Ptolemy studied the planets from Alexandria. He believed the Earth was the centre of the universe as he showed in this diagram.

The Alexandrians were interested in geography. This is the scientist Eratosthenes who used the angle of the sun's shadow to work out the distance round the Earth.

Siege catapult

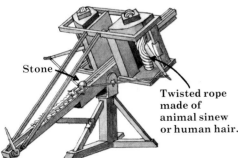

Stone

Twisted rope made of animal sinew or human hair.

Alexander's military engineers designed catapults, which hurled stones, for attacking walled cities. Later, the Romans used catapults in their sieges too.

How to make a catapult

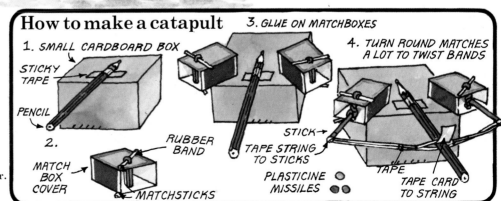

1. SMALL CARDBOARD BOX
STICKY TAPE
PENCIL

2.
MATCH BOX COVER
RUBBER BAND
MATCHSTICKS

3. GLUE ON MATCHBOXES

4. TURN ROUND MATCHES A LOT TO TWIST BANDS
STICK
TAPE STRING TO STICKS
PLASTICINE MISSILES
TAPE
TAPE CARD TO STRING

Stick a pencil to a small box, like this. Make holes through two matchbox covers, push through short rubber bands. Slide match sticks through them. Glue covers to the box.

Push two sticks into the bands. Tape string to the ends. Tape the string on each side of the pencil and a bit of card on top. Wind round the match sticks. Load and pull back to fire.

What We Owe the Greeks

We know more about the Greeks than many earlier people, because they wrote proper histories. Other people listed kings' names and events, but did not try to explain things. The Greek historian, Herodotus, wrote studies of people and their customs. Thucydides, who fought in the Peloponnesian War, wrote a detailed history of the war and its causes. Besides the writing of history, we have inherited many other things from the Greeks, including ideas of politics, theatre and many words.

The Greeks developed the art of thinking about problems. They called this philosophy. Two of the world's greatest philosophers, Socrates and Plato, lived in Athens.

Some scholars, like Aristotle, studied scientific problems. He carefully watched animals and realised that the porpoise was a mammal not a fish when he saw it give birth to live babies.

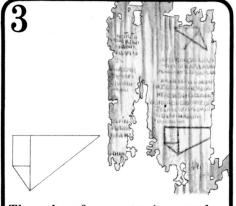

The rules of geometry invented by Greeks such as Euclid and Pythagoras are still used today. This Greek papyrus shows how to solve a problem in geometry.

The Greeks studied plants. Manuscripts, like this, record recipes for medicines made of plants. Alexander sent rare plants from the East to Aristotle.

Chariot racing

The Olympic Games

Greek festivals held in honour of the gods included competitions in sports, music and drama. Some of these "games" lasted several days. The games at Corinth and the Pythian Games at Delphi were both important, but the most famous were the Olympic Games held every four years at the great sanctuary of the god Zeus at Olympia.

The competitors had to be free Greeks, not slaves, and they swore an oath to keep the rules. All wars in Greece had to stop while the games were in progress. At the end of the games, oxen were sacrificed to Zeus and everyone joined in a great feast.

Discus

Temple of Zeus

This athlete is about to throw a round bronze weight called the discus. The winner is the man who throws it furthest.

Art and architecture

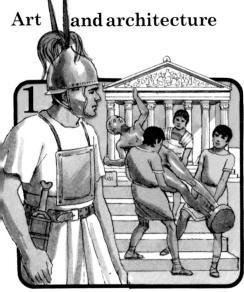

1 When the Romans conquered Greece, their generals carried off many works of art. The Romans admired Greek statues so much that they had marble copies made.

2 After the fall of the Roman empire, statues were buried and lost. In the 15th century AD, people began to be interested in the ancient world and dug up the remains.

3 From then on, architects throughout Europe revived Greek and Roman styles of building. Today, most cities have some public buildings which are in the "Classical" style.

Throwing the javelin. It was hurled from a leather thong wrapped round the athlete's fingers.

Four-horse racing was part of the Olympic Games, but it took place on a separate race-track called the hippodrome. The Romans took over this exciting sport from the Greeks.

Wrestling

Judge with his official rod

This is a sprint race. There were also races run by men wearing full armour.

Spot the columns

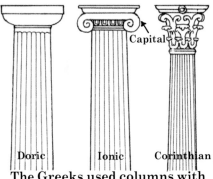

Doric   Ionic   Corinthian

Capital

The Greeks used columns with decorated tops (capitals) to support the roofs of their temples. You may be able to spot these columns on present-day buildings.

Key dates

499	Ionian Greeks revolted against Persian rule.
490	Start of Persian wars. Persians defeated at Battle of Marathon.
480	Greeks defeated at Thermopylae, then victorious at Salamis.
478/477	Athens led league of Greek states.
462/429	**Pericles,** leader at Athens.
431/404	**Peloponnesian War** between Sparta and Athens.
338	**Philip II** of Macedon won control of Greece.
336/323	**Reign of Alexander the Great.** During this time Alexander won a huge empire. On his death, the empire was divided up by his successors.

Approximate BC dates.

Great Civilisation in the East

Until 221BC, China was divided into several rival states. Then, the king of a state called Ch'in defeated them all and became the First Emperor of all China. "Shih Huang Ti", as he was called, was the first of a family line of emperors (a dynasty) called the Ch'in emperors.

Later, a new dynasty of emperors—the Han emperors—ruled China. During their time, General Chang Chien was sent to the West to find allies. As a result of his travels, a new trade route, called the Silk Road, was opened up.

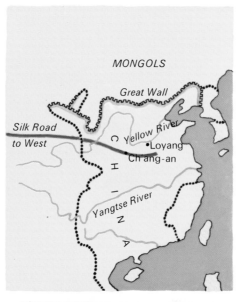

Key dates

551/479BC	The great thinker **Confucius**.
463/221BC	Period of the warring states.
221BC	China unified under **Shih Huang Ti**, the first emperor. Great Wall built. Beginning of Ch'in Dynasty. Standard bronze coins introduced.
206BC/AD220	Han Dynasty.
200BC*	Paper invented. Beginnings of Chinese civil service.

***These dates are approximate**

When the people of China were counted in AD2, there were about 60 million. Most were peasants who grew rice, their most important crop, on specially built terraces.

The great lords had huge tombs built for themselves for a comfortable life-after-death. This princess's body was covered with jade, which was thought to preserve it.

The emperor was the supreme lord. He controlled the salt wells, which were vital to people far from the sea. Bamboo tubes were drilled down 400 metres into the brine.

How we know

Peasant's cottage

Peasant girl

We can learn a great deal about life at the time of the Han emperors from the pottery models placed in tombs. This is a simple one-storey house a peasant might live in.

Farm

Watch tower

Farm animals

In troubled times, even a farm needed towers to watch for barbarians or soldiers. A rich lord had models of servants and soldiers in his tomb to impress the gods.

Bronze figure of tall Western horse

General Chang Chien brought back a new breed of horses from the West. The big, strong horses were very useful against the small ponies ridden by the barbarians.

The Great Wall

The Great Wall of China was built by Shih Huang Ti when he became emperor. He joined together short sections of wall put up by earlier warlords to keep raiding tribes out of their lands. The wall still stands and is 2,710km long.

Beacons on the watch towers signal the approach of an enemy.

A convoy on the Silk Road is halted by an attack.

Chinese cross-bowman

Barbarians on their swift ponies.

The wall is wide enough to take chariots.

Silk

Silkworm

Sorting cocoons

The Chinese made and sold fine silk. They kept silk worms (caterpillars of the silk moth), which spin cocoons of fine silk thread. They dyed and wove this silk into cloth.

Patterns of plants and animals were woven into the silk. This lion pattern may have been borrowed from Persia, which shows ideas as well as goods were taken along the Silk Road.

Money

Fish money

Standard money

Silk

Silk was so valuable it could be used for payment. Bronze coins in strange shapes were also used. Later, round coins with square holes became the standard money.

Writing and Inventions

1 The Chinese emperor was treated almost like a god by his millions of subjects. He had armies of officials and soldiers to run his empire. The officials—civil servants—collected taxes and looked after roads.

2 People who wanted to be civil servants had to take exams. Any boy who could read and write had a chance. But he had to know large amounts of ancient poetry and the teachings of the great thinker, Confucius.

3 Confucius was born in 551BC. He taught that the emperor should be like a father to his people who should love and obey him. Confucian scholars had to be good at music, arithmetic, archery and chess.

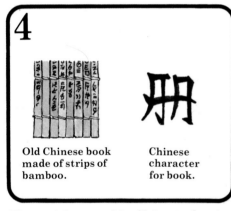

Old Chinese book made of strips of bamboo.

Chinese character for book.

4 The writing used in China today is thousands of years old. Each character was based on a picture. Gradually the pictures became simple brush strokes.

5 The ancient Chinese wrote and painted on long pieces of silk. They used Chinese brushes and ground up a solid block of ink on a stone with a little water.

6 The Chinese painted pictures in beautiful colours. In a corner, they often put the characters which were based on things in the picture, such as "mountain" and "river".

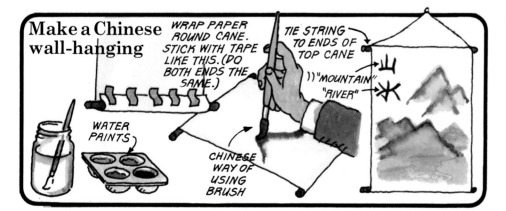

Make a Chinese wall-hanging

WRAP PAPER ROUND CANE. STICK WITH TAPE LIKE THIS. (DO BOTH ENDS THE SAME.)

WATER PAINTS

CHINESE WAY OF USING BRUSH

TIE STRING TO ENDS OF TOP CANE

"MOUNTAIN"
"RIVER"

You will need a piece of paper about foolscap size. Fasten a piece of cane at each end with sticky tape. Hold your brush in the Chinese way and paint a landscape picture, using the Chinese painting above as a guide. Next copy the Chinese characters. These are the characters for "river" and "mountain". Together they mean "landscape".

Inventions

At first the Chinese wrote on costly silk or in heavy bamboo books. Later, they began making paper from bark and hemp. This was used for writing, painting and taking rubbings from stone tablets.

Life in the city

All the cities built at the time of the Han emperors have disappeared. This picture of their capital city, Ch'ang-An, is based on details from paintings, sculptures and tomb figures made at the time.

A rich merchant lives in this splendid painted house with his family and slaves.

An elegant procession of court officials.

A scholar teaches his pupils the ideas of Confucius. People respect scholars much more than rich merchants.

House walls are lacquered to make them waterproof.

People buy food at market stalls.

A government official rides in his carriage. He is very important and people have to jump out of the way.

2

The Chinese invented the first compass. A spoon-shaped piece of magnetic stone, called lode stone, was placed on a polished bronze board. The spoon turned until it pointed to the North Pole.

3

The Chinese covered wooden bowls and boxes with layers of sticky resin, called lacquer, from the lac tree. They lacquered their shoes, chariots and umbrellas to make them waterproof and colourful.

4

This is an instrument for detecting earthquakes. The slightest tremor in the earth tilts the carefully balanced mechanism inside. Then a dragon's jaws open and a ball falls into a toad's mouth.

Nomads and Horsemen

Between the civilisations of the Mediterranean and China were vast treeless plains and mountains. The tribes living there wandered great distances to find pasture for their horses and cattle.

One tribe, the Mongols, sometimes attacked the Great Wall of China. Another, the Scythians, were described by the Greek historian, Herodotus, as fine horsemen and archers. Russians digging in the Altai found tombs built about 500BC with objects preserved in ice.

MONGOLS

ALTAI

SCYTHS

ARAL SEA

BLACK SEA

CASPIAN SEA

PERSIANS

Zagros Mountains

CHINA

Himalayas

RED SEA

PERSIAN GULF

INDIA

Scythian horse-breeders

The Scythians of the Altai roamed the plains during the summer months but lived in log cabins **during the winter. They sold horses from their huge herds to the Chinese and Persians.**

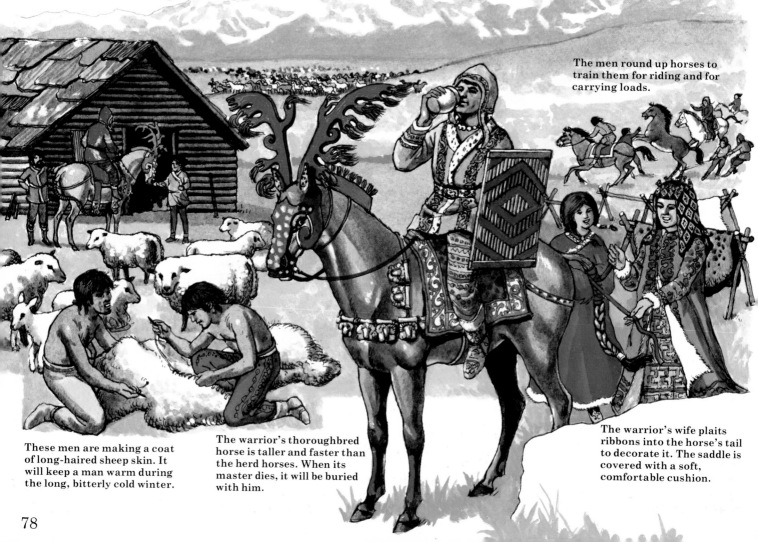

The men round up horses to train them for riding and for carrying loads.

These men are making a coat of long-haired sheep skin. It will keep a man warm during the long, bitterly cold winter.

The warrior's thoroughbred horse is taller and faster than the herd horses. When its master dies, it will be buried with him.

The warrior's wife plaits ribbons into the horse's tail to decorate it. The saddle is covered with a soft, comfortable cushion.

Inside a Scythian cabin

During the winter, the Scythians made things of felt, with cut-out shapes sewn on them, called appliqué. They also stitched embroidery. All their belongings were made so that they could be packed on to horses when they moved on.

How to do appliqué

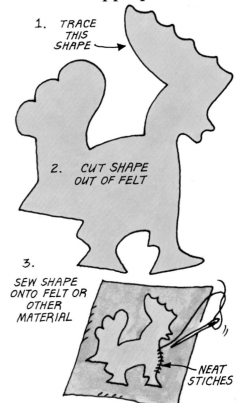

1. TRACE THIS SHAPE

2. CUT SHAPE OUT OF FELT

3. SEW SHAPE ONTO FELT OR OTHER MATERIAL

NEAT STICHES

Trace this shape of this Scythian cockerel and cut it out of coloured felt or material. Stitch it to a large piece of felt or cloth. Sew on more cut-out shapes to make a wall hanging.

1 Mongols

The Mongols were true nomads and wandered the whole year round. Their tents, called yurts, were made of animal hair felt, waterproofed with fat, and held up by wooden frames.

2

Mongol chieftains had very large yurts, comfortably furnished inside. They loaded them on to large carts, pulled by teams of oxen, when it was time to drive their herds on again.

How we know

The Scythians made things of gold, such as this plaque. It may show a warrior's death.

3

When ponies were needed from the herd, men caught them with lassoos on poles. The men made a special drink of mares' milk but most work was done by women.

4

Water was so precious to the Mongols when travelling that no cooking pots or clothes were allowed to be washed. Visitors to a camp had to walk between fires to be purified.

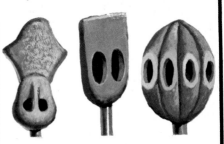

The Mongols made whistles, like these to join to arrows. They could hear where an arrow fell.

Early American Indians

The first "Indians" of North America ate seeds and berries, and followed herds of wild animals. Later, they began to build more permanent homes and grow crops near them.

Some, like the Hopewell people, built large cemeteries for their dead. In Central America the Indians began to build pyramids. At first they faced them with clay and later with stone slabs. Ideas and knowledge spread, partly when they traded with each other, back from Mexico to the Indians of North America.

NORTHERN FOREST TRIBES

NORTH AMERICA

CENTRAL AMERICA

TRIBES OF THE GREAT PLAINS

EASTERN WOODLAND TRIBES

SOUTH WEST DESERT TRIBES

Serpent Mound

SOUTH EAST AND FLORIDA TRIBES

SOUTH WEST MESA TRIBES

ATLANTIC OCEAN

Teotihuacan

PACIFIC OCEAN

OLMECS

MEXICO

MAYA

Copan

The Indians of the desert lived in caves and went out hunting for wild sheep. They wove elaborate baskets and the mocassins they made of skins have been found.

On the plains and in the woodlands, the Indians lived in shallow pit houses, covered with hides. A holy man, called a shaman, chanted spells to cure ill people.

Some of the woodland tribes built huge mounds of earth in the shape of animals. This snake is about 500 metres long and was made by Hopewell Indians 2,000 years ago.

Olmec Indians in Central America built huge stone statues. This one is three metres high. They thought their jaguar-god mated with women, who had half-jaguar babies.

A city of pyramids was built at Teotihuacan in Central Mexico. Round the city were fields of maize, beans and pumpkins to feed about 200,000 people who lived there.

Maize god   Maize plant

The Indians of North America learned how to grow tobacco from the people in Central America. They also grew maize, which came from Mexico. It was such a good food, they made it a god.

The Maya

The Maya Indians of Central America built cities which can still be seen deep in the jungle. They were a very religious people and worshipped rain, earth, plant and animal gods. They played a religious ball game in specially built courts. Priests helped the players to dress and kept score.

The Maya studied the moon, stars and planets, and had a complicated calendar for counting the days and years. They wanted to predict when such frightening things as an eclipse of the sun would happen.

The ball court at Copan

How to play hip ball

A player tosses the ball over the line. The teams hit it across the line, using only hips, thighs and elbows. A point is scored against the one who lets it drop. The first to score 21 wins the game.

The ball court at Copan was probably built late in the eighth century AD. The players, bandaged to prevent injuries, used a solid rubber ball.

They bounced the ball backwards and forwards, using only their hips, thighs and elbows, but not their feet. No one really knows how they scored goals.

How we know

We know very little about how the Maya people lived. This tomb painting shows they fought their neighbours, probably to capture people to sacrifice to the gods.

The Maya were very good stone carvers. These masons are working on a giant pillar, probably showing a king, which will be set up to mark an important date in the calendar.

Maya pot showing bat god.

Mayan potters made marvellous pots of clay. They coiled long strips of clay round and round, to build up the pot. The man here turns the pot round with his feet.

Life in Ancient Africa

The first people lived in Africa about three million years ago. From the great civilisations of Egypt, other Africans learned how to work gold, copper, tin and bronze.

The Assyrians, with iron weapons, invaded the Nile valley in 671BC and the use of iron spread. Two powerful kingdoms grew up south of Egypt—Kush and Axum (modern Ethiopia). Christianity was brought to Ethiopia by Egyptian monks. King Ezana was one of the first rulers to become a Christian.

Key dates

1000BC*	Beginnings of Kingdom of Kush. Capital at Napata.
751/664BC	Kushite kings conquered and and ruled Egypt.
671BC	The Asyrians invaded the Nile Valley.
590BC*	Capital of Kush moved from Napata to Meroe.
AD339	Meroe conquered by King Ezana of Axum.

*These dates are approximate.

Some of Africa's earliest history can be seen in paintings on the walls of caves. This picture, based on a rock painting, shows a battle between small bushmen and tall

Bantu warriors. Such battles between the tribes forced the weaker ones to move their herds and villages to new areas where no people had ever lived before.

The capital of the kingdom of Kush was at Napata until about 590BC. Then a new capital was built at Meroe, near iron deposits. It had pyramid tombs like those in Egypt.

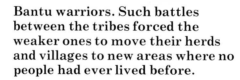

The working of iron probably spread from the kingdom of Kush westwards across Africa. Black-smiths became important because they knew how to make weapons.

The North African coast had been settled by Phoenicians and Greeks. The Romans then went further inland. Nomads in the hills learned to trade at markets.

The traders of Axum exchanged their goods at the port of Adulis. Spices came from India and Ceylon, and cloth from the Roman empire. Romans, Greeks and Arabs bought African ivory.

Buddha and Ashoka

People called the Aryans moved into India in about 1750BC but little is known of India's history at that time. After the conquests of Alexander the Great in Northern India and Pakistan, a line of kings, the Mauryas, built a great empire. They learned ideas of government from the Greeks and Persians. Ashoka, a Mauryan conqueror, was converted to Buddhism and made it the state religion. Beautiful art and sculpture developed under the next strong line of kings, the Guptas.

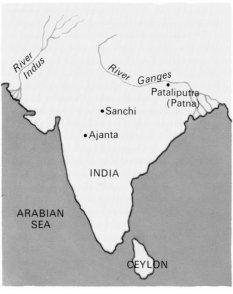

Key dates

560/480BC **Gautama** (The Buddha)
327/325BC Campaigns of Alexander the Great in India and Pakistan.
321/185BC The Mauryan Dynasty founded by **Chandragupta**.
272/231BC **Ashoka,** grandson of Chandragupta, was emperor. Capital city at Pataliputra (modern Patna). Buddhism spread through India.
AD320/535 The Gupta empire.
AD400/500 The Ajanta frescoes were painted.

1 Vishnu one of the many Hindu gods.

The Aryans' religion was Hinduism. Priests taught that the gods decided which way of life, or caste, a person was born into. A good man might be reborn into a better caste.

2 There were four castes, but many people, like those here, were too lowly to be in any of them. They were called "untouchables" and did the worst jobs.

3 The high caste rulers of India lived in great luxury in their palaces. This fresco, painted on a cave wall at Ajanta in about AD400, shows the inside of a palace.

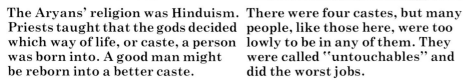

1 Buddha

Gautama, a young prince, was so moved when he saw suffering people, he left his father's palace to find a better way of life.

2 He went to live in a forest as a holy man and thought out a kinder religion. He became known as the Buddha, which means the enlightened one.

3 People listened to the Buddha and his ideas spread. Later, great earth mounds, called stupas, were built in places where he had preached.

4 Top of one of Ashoka's columns.

The Buddha's teachings were adopted by the great Emperor Ashoka. He made fairer laws which were written on stone columns.

People of Northern Europe

The Celtic tribes moved out from their homelands in north Europe and settled over a wide area. They were fierce warriors, who won the respect of the Greeks and the Romans. Julius Caesar had to fight many hard battles between 58 and 51BC to conquer the Celts in Gaul (now approximately modern France).

The Celts in Britain were not conquered until the invasion of Emperor Claudius in AD43. Even then, they kept their own languages which, in places, still survive today.

A chief shows how brave he is by fighting without his helmet.

Prisoners of war are sold as slaves. Britain was a good source of slaves for the Romans.

At home

The Celts lived in thatched, wooden huts and wove wool in tartan patterns for clothes. Their craftsmen were very skilled at making wonderful objects in bronze and gold. Their bards made up great poems which they recited from memory.

Farming

The Celts in Gaul invented a reaping machine, which was copied by the Romans. They stored their grain for the winter in pits. Hunting wild boar, their favourite food, was a great sport. The children played a game rather like hockey.

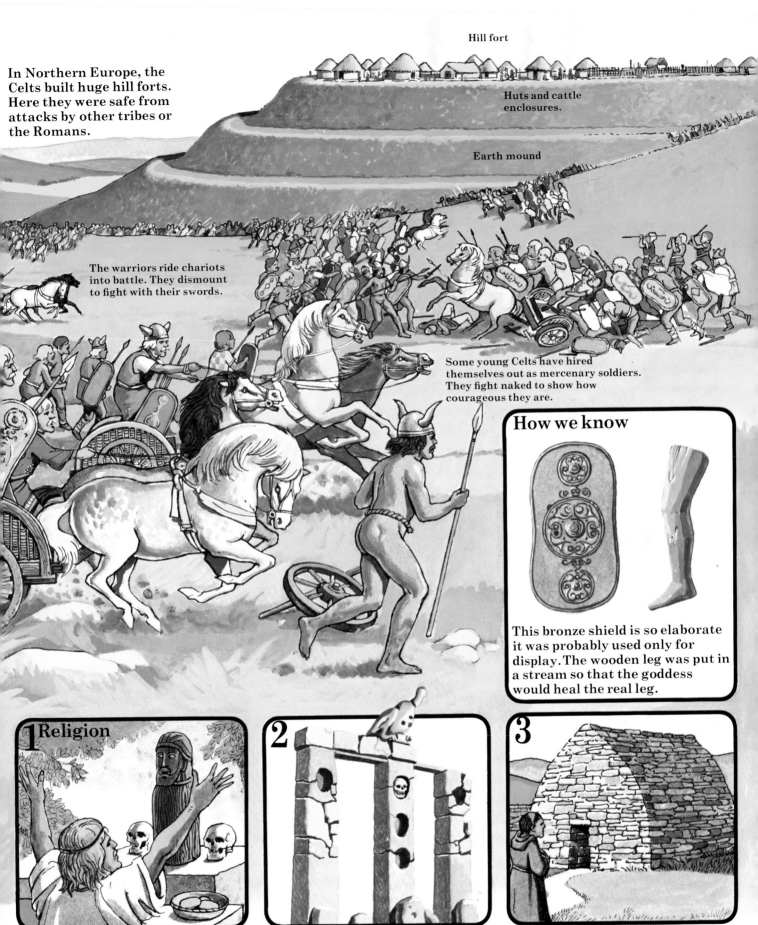

In Northern Europe, the Celts built huge hill forts. Here they were safe from attacks by other tribes or the Romans.

Hill fort

Huts and cattle enclosures.

Earth mound

The warriors ride chariots into battle. They dismount to fight with their swords.

Some young Celts have hired themselves out as mercenary soldiers. They fight naked to show how courageous they are.

How we know

This bronze shield is so elaborate it was probably used only for display. The wooden leg was put in a stream so that the goddess would heal the real leg.

1 Religion

The Celts had priests, called Druids. It took many years to become a Druid. He had to train his memory so he could learn, and hand on, the laws and customs of the tribes.

2

Human skulls were placed in this monument at Roquepertuse, France. Human remains, probably from sacrifices, have been found in pits at some religious centres of the Celts.

3

Later the Celts became Christians. They set up communities of monks in remote parts of Ireland and Scotland. Some, such as St Columba, were sent to convert the heathens.

The Rise of Rome

1

The city of Rome began as a small village on one of seven hills. More villages were built until they joined up into one big town.

2

At first Rome was ruled by kings, the last of whom was an Etruscan. Later, the people rebelled and set up a "republic" (a state without a king).

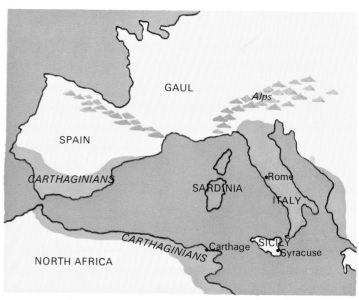

3

The Romans conquered other peoples in Italy. They fought the Carthaginians whose leader, Hannibal, invaded Italy in 218BC.

4

Men who fought for Rome settled down to farm the land they had conquered. They brought the Roman way of life to the provinces.

5

People captured in battle were made Roman slaves. One called Spartacus, who was trained as a gladiator, led a slave revolt in 71BC.

The Etruscans

Etruscan man and woman from top of coffin.

The Etruscan people lived in central Italy. Little is known about them and their writings cannot be read. Their sculpture shows Greek influence.

Roman roads

Roman soldiers built thousands of miles of good roads. Troops could march quickly along them to control the huge empire they had captured.

Flat stones

Rubble

Stones

Ditch

The end of the Republic

1 In Rome many men plotted to gain control and there were civil wars. Julius Caesar, a great general, marched his army to Rome in 49BC.

2 Caesar soon gained power and brought peace. But one group, fearing he planned to make himself king, stabbed him to death on the Ides (the 15th) of March 44BC.

3 There were more civil wars until Octavian, Caesar's heir, defeated his rival, Mark Antony. Antony and his wife, Cleopatra, Queen of Egypt, killed themselves.

4 Octavian was given the title Augustus and later became the first emperor of Rome. He restored order in the army and revived old Roman customs.

The Roman army

The well-trained Roman armies spread outwards from Rome, gradually winning more and more territory. The soldiers laid siege to enemy forts, marching up to the walls under a roof of shields. They built wooden towers to scale the walls and broke down gates with a battering ram, roofed with skins.

When marching through enemy lands, the soldiers set up a camp each night. They rounded up animals and cut crops for food.

They used catapults to fling huge stones on to the defenders. A soldier carried the standard which was crowned by the legion's eagle.

87

Life in the Roman Empire

The rule of Emperor Augustus brought an end to the Roman republic with elected leaders. In its place, a peaceful empire was set up.

Inside the well-guarded Roman frontiers, new cities grew up where no towns had been before. Fine temples and houses of brick or stone were built in all parts of the empire, from Britain to North Africa. The people in the provinces traded for the goods they needed and paid government taxes for the upkeep of the army.

Gladiator fights

People flocked to the big arenas, called amphitheatres, in the cities. There they watched fights to the death between gladiators and wild animals or condemned criminals.

Country life

Although there were many towns and cities, most people lived in the country. Rich men had large estates, looked after for them by farmers who paid them rents with money, food or animals. On the estates were grand houses, called villas, where the rich families lived with their servants and slaves. Workers on the estates grew vegetables, wheat, fruit, grapes for making wine, and olives for oil. They kept hens and geese, cows, sheep and goats. Oil and wine were stored in big pottery jars half-buried in the courtyard.

In the cities, fresh water was brought from the hills by aqueducts. Then it flowed along lead pipes to street fountains and houses. There were baths where people could wash and swim. Food and wine were shipped from the provinces to the city docks.

Streets were paved with stone and had drains to keep them clean.

Aqueduct

Baths

Wheat from the provinces.

Statue of emperor

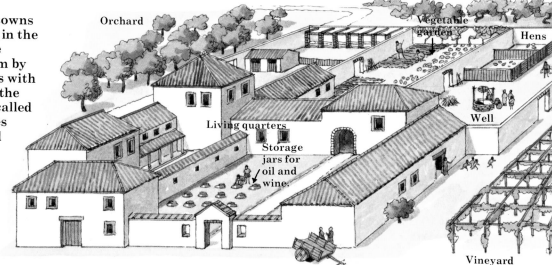

Orchard

Vegetable garden

Hens

Living quarters

Storage jars for oil and wine.

Well

Vineyard

Amphitheatre

Temple

Laws were carved on stone plaques on the walls.

Roman coins

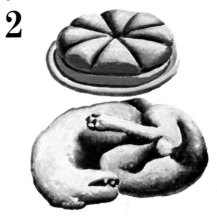

The Romans had many different coins, made by the government. The pictures on them were often of an event or new law.

Pompeii

1

A volcano, called Mount Vesuvius, towers over the Bay of Naples in Italy. In AD79, it erupted, sending choking fumes and ashes down on the towns at its base. The city of Pompeii was buried by rivers of scorching lava.

Archaeologists have now dug through the lava and found the city. It is a record of Roman life, preserved in great detail.

2

The shape of a round loaf of bread, still on a plate, was preserved by the lava. Some people and animals choked to death in the fumes. This dog was chained up when it died.

Mosaics were used to decorate the floors of the villas. Often they show scenes from country life like this farmer digging the soil around his grape vines.

The ordinary people had very little of their own. They grew what food they could on rented land for their families and for sale. This man is driving his cow to a city market.

3

Many houses, with coloured paintings on their walls, have been found under the lava. Some paintings, like this one, were portraits of people who lived there.

Romans and Barbarians

After Augustus, the Roman empire was ruled well by strong emperors. Armies guarded its frontiers and many people became its citizens. From the time of Emperor Marcus Aurelius, however, the empire was troubled by barbarian invasions. The Roman armies grew more powerful and began to set up their own leaders as emperors, which led to civil wars. Eventually Emperor Diocletian divided the empire into four parts, each with its own capital city.

1 Hadrian's Wall

In the Roman provinces, forts protected the frontiers. Emperor Hadrian had forts, linked by a huge wall, built across northern England to keep out the barbarians.

2 Shapur
Roman emperor

Rome's old enemies, the Persians, attacked the frontiers, led by Shapur. Emperor Valerian marched against him but was defeated and captured at Edessa in AD260.

3

The emperors tried to pay for larger armies by minting extra money. Bronze coins were coated with silver to look more valuable. People needed sacks of them to pay their taxes.

4

People wanted to blame someone for the empire's troubles. They picked on the Christians who would not worship Roman gods. Thousands were killed in the arenas.

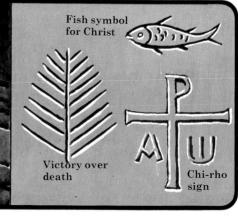

5

Tribes searching for new land invaded Northern Italy. Emperor Aurelian drove them out and had walls built round Rome as the empire's centre was no longer safe.

The Jews

Jar in which scroll was kept.

Dead Sea scroll.

Jews in Palestine rebelled against the Romans, who destroyed Jerusalem in AD70. One group lived in caves near the Dead Sea and hid their religious writings there.

The Christians

Some people in Palestine followed a religious leader called Jesus. They were known as Christians because he was called Christ, the Messiah, and met secretly in catacombs

Fish symbol for Christ

Victory over death

Chi-rho sign

The Christians used secret symbols. The fish was a symbol for Christ. The Chi-rho sign is the first two letters of Christ in Greek. The palm leaf means victory over death.

The empire splits up

Statue of the Tetrarchs which now stands in Venice.

1 Wars on several frontiers made the empire difficult to control. Emperor Diocletian divided it into four parts, each with a ruler, or "tetrarch"; two junior and two senior.

2 Diocletian's successors fought for power. Constantine beat his rival at the Milvian Bridge in Rome. He had dreamed he would win if he carried the Christian symbol.

3 Constantine then became a Christian and set up a new capital, called after him at the old Greek city of Byzantium. Later Emperor Theodosius II built walls round it.

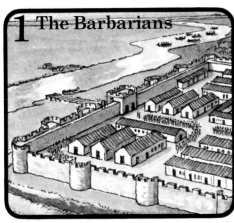

1 The Barbarians People in the Roman empire asked barbarians to protect them against other barbarians. But the attacks went on. In Britain, forts and look-out towers were built to guard the coasts.

2 Roman emperors, in need of good soldiers, paid barbarians to lead their armies. Stilicho, a Vandal, commanded all troops and married the niece of Theodosius I.

3 The fiercest barbarians, the Huns, came from central Asia and had driven many people into Roman lands. Their leader, Attila, was called "the scourge of God".

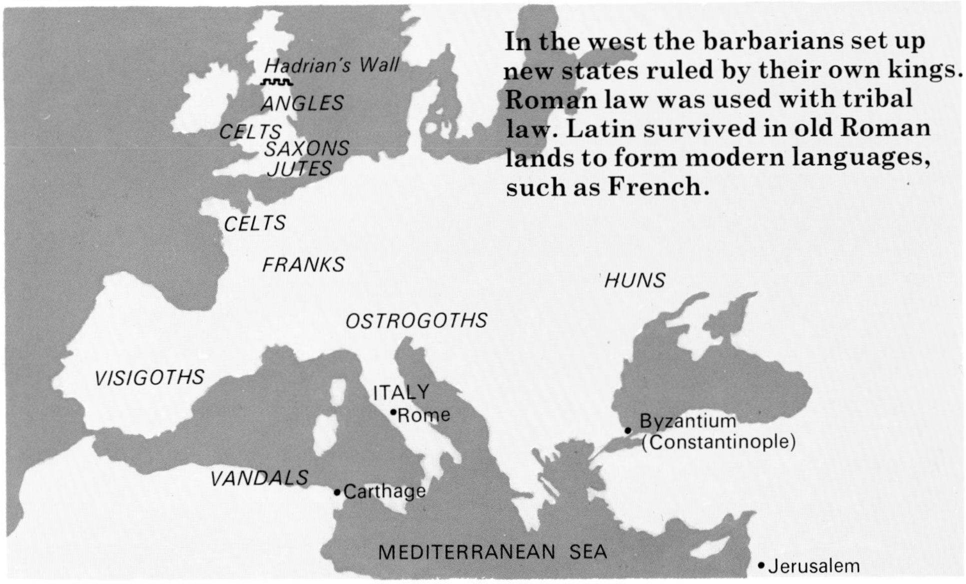

People in the Roman empire asked barbarians to protect them against other barbarians. But the attacks went on. In Britain, forts and look-out towers were built to guard the coasts.

In the west the barbarians set up new states ruled by their own kings. Roman law was used with tribal law. Latin survived in old Roman lands to form modern languages, such as French.

Map labels: Hadrian's Wall, ANGLES, CELTS, SAXONS, JUTES, CELTS, FRANKS, HUNS, OSTROGOTHS, VISIGOTHS, ITALY, Rome, Byzantium (Constantinople), VANDALS, Carthage, MEDITERRANEAN SEA, Jerusalem

Buried treasure

The Romans often buried their treasures to hide them from attacking barbarians. These Christian silver objects, which are about 1,600 years old, were dug up in a field in England.

The Byzantine Empire

The city of Constantinople resisted attacks by barbarians and became the capital of the eastern half of the Roman empire. This eastern empire lasted for more than 1,000 years and is called the Byzantine empire.

In the sixth century AD, some land captured by the barbarians was won back. The armies of Emperor Justinian regained Italy from the Ostrogoths and North Africa from the Vandals. But there were costly wars with the rival Persian empire.

The court of Justinian

Justinian's wife Theodora was a clever and powerful woman who helped rule.

The imperial guards have Christian signs on their shields.

Silk for robes worn by rich people came only from China and the Persians made trade difficult. Monks, so the story goes, brought silk worms to Justinian to start a silk industry.

The Romans decorated the walls and floors of their houses with small cubes of coloured stone. These are called mosaics. At the time of Justinian, coloured glass, sometimes with gold set in it, was used, and even precious stones.

How to make a mosaic

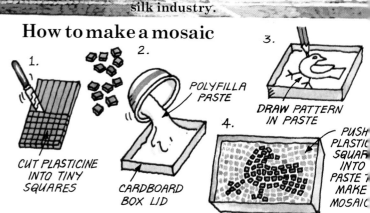

1. CUT PLASTICINE INTO TINY SQUARES

2. POLYFILLA PASTE / CARDBOARD BOX LID

3. DRAW PATTERN IN PASTE

4. PUSH PLASTIC SQUARE INTO PASTE TO MAKE MOSAIC

Roll out plasticine and cut it into tiny squares (1). Mix Polyfilla with water to make a thick paste and pour it into a small box lid (2). Draw a picture in the paste (3). Before the paste sets, push the coloured plasticine squares into it to make a mosaic, like this (4)

Chariot race

Many customs were brought from Rome. Chariot racing in the circus became mixed with politics. In a great riot, 30,000 supporters of the Blue and Green parties were killed.

The earliest Christian monks built monasteries in Egypt. Some wanted to live alone in great discomfort to prove their faith. One monk, Simon, spent years on a pillar.

In the monasteries, monks copied out manuscripts of Christian writings and older Greek works. They kept up the skills of painting ikons (images) of holy people.

Barbarian kingdoms

KINGDOM OF THE FRANKS

KINGDOM OF THE VISIGOTHS

OSTROGOTHS

ITALY
•Rome

Constantinople

PERSIANS

BYZANTINE EMPIRE
at the time of Justinian

MEDITERRANEAN SEA

King Recceswinth's crown

His name

Justinian's empire is shown here. In the west are the beginnings of several European kingdoms. The Franks have settled in France and Germany, and the Visigoths in Spain.

The Visigoths were a Germanic people. This crown was put in a church as an offering by King Recceswinth. It may have been made by Byzantine craftsmen.

The Ostrogoths settled in Italy and were finally defeated by Justinian. They made jewellery in eagle designs. The Anglo-Saxon gold cross was worn as a Christian symbol.

Key dates

753BC	Traditional date of founding of Rome.
575BC	Rome ruled by Etruscan kings.
509BC	Romans set up republic.
264/241BC	First war with Carthage.
218BC	Second war with Carthage. **Hannibal** crossed the Pyrenees.
200BC	Rome began conquest of eastern Mediterranean.
146BC	Romans destroyed Carthage and Corinth.
73/71BC	**Spartacus** led slave revolt.
58–51BC	**Julius Caesar** conquered Celts in Gaul.
44BC	**Julius Caesar** murdered in Rome.
30BC	**Antony and Cleopatra** committed suicide.
27BC	**Octavian** called Augustus; beginning of Roman Empire.
AD14	Death of **Augustus**.
AD70	Temple at Jerusalem destroyed.
AD79	Eruption of Vesuvius; Pompeii destroyed.
AD117/38	**Hadrian** was emperor; built wall across north of England.
AD161/180	**Marcus Aurelius** was emperor.
AD235	Barbarian invasions and civil wars began.
AD249/250	First persecution of Christians under Emperor **Decius**.
AD270/275	**Aurelian** was emperor; built wall round city of Rome.
AD285/305	**Diocletian** was emperor.
AD312	**Constantine** won battle of Milvian Bridge.
AD330	Dedication of city of Constantinople.
AD395	Division of Roman empire into East and West.
AD527/565	**Justinian** was emperor.

Time Chart:
First Civilisations to the Fall of Rome

	Mesopotamia and Persia	Egypt	Africa	Mediterranean lands of Europe
	Development of farming. Rise of city-states in Sumer. Pottery being made.	Development of farming. Pottery being made. Hieroglyphs invented.	Rock drawings in middle of Sahara showing animals and people.	Stone monuments built, eg in Malta.
	Cuneiform writing invented.			
	Wheel invented.			
3000BC	Early Dynastic period in Sumer (First 2 dynasties of rulers). Royal graves of Ur.	Unification of Egypt. ARCHAIC PERIOD in Egypt. OLD KINGDOM. Step Pyramids built.		EARLY MINOAN PERIOD in Crete.
2500BC	**Sargon** of Akkad. The Gutians invade. Dynasty III of Ur.	Straight-sided pyramids built.		
2000BC	Arrival of the Amorites. Rise of Babylon. Reign of King **Hammurabi** of Babylon. Rise of Assyria, under King **Shamsi-Adad I.**	MIDDLE KINGDOM. Conquest of Nubia. Invasion by Hyksos.		MIDDLE MINOAN PERIOD in Crete. Picture writing (hieroglyphs) in use in Crete. Palaces built in Crete. LATE MINOAN PERIOD in Crete. Rise of Mycenaeans in Greece.
1500BC	Kassites rule Babylon.  The Mitanni rule in northern Mesopotamia. Arrival of the Persians.	NEW KINGDOM. Conquest of empire. Valley of Kings in use. Warrior pharaohs in power. **Queen Hatshepsut.** **Tutankhamun**		Eruption of Thera. Linear B writing in use in Crete. Fall of Crete, destruction of Palace of Knossos.
1000BC	Rise and fall of ASSYRIAN EMPIRE. Rise of NEW BABYLONIAN EMPIRE. Rule of **Nebuchadnezzar** in Babylon. Birth of prophet **Zarathushtra.**	LATE PERIOD Slow decline. Invasion by Assyrians and Kushites.	Beginnings of Kingdom of Kush. Spread of iron working. Carthage founded by Phoenician princess **Dido.** Capital of Kush moved to Meroe.	Decline of Mycenaeans. Arrival of Dorians in Greece. DARK AGES in Greece. Greek poet **Homer** alive. Etruscans in Northern Italy. Traditional date of founding of Rome 753BC City-states in Greece.
500BC	PERSIAN EMPIRE at its height. Conquests of **Alexander the Great** (including Persian empire).	Egyptian revival Conquest by Persia, then Alexander the Great. Rule of the Ptolemies. **Cleopatra.**	Carthage at war with Rome (Punic wars). **Hannibal.** Carthage defeated. North Africa part of Roman empire.	Persian wars between Greeks and Persians. City of Athens very powerful. Peloponnesian War in Greece. Rule of **Pericles** in Athens. **Alexander the Great.** Rise of Rome. **Julius Caesar.**
0	SASSANIAN EMPIRE	Conquest by Rome. Part of Roman Empire.	Meroe conquered by **King Ezana** of Axum. Slow movement of people across central and southern Africa. Arrival of barbarians (Vandals) in North Africa.	**Augustus,** Roman emperor. ROMAN EMPIRE. Spread of Christianity. Split of Roman empire into West and East. BYZANTINE EMPIRE. Byzantine empire ruled by Emperor **Justinian.**
AD500		Hieroglyphs fall into disuse.		

Northern Europe	Western Asia	India	China	America
Stone monuments built in northern and western Europe. 	First farmers. First cities—Jericho and Catal Hüyük. 		Early farming communities growing millet.	
		Rise of Indus Valley People.		Farmers growing cotton. Maize grown in Mexico. 
	Several independent states in Anatolia. Arrival of Assyrian merchants for trade. Arrival of Canaanites in Eastern Mediterranean lands.	Cities like Mohenjo-Daro and Harappa built. Writing in use.		Pottery being made.
Stonehenge built.  Spread of skilled bronze working.	Hittites arrive in Anatolia. 	Decline of Indus Valley people. Arrival of Aryan People.		
	HITTITE EMPIRE Arrival of Sea Peoples. 	Development of caste system. Growth of Hindu religion.	SHANG DYNASTY. Development of skilled bronze working. 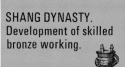 Royal tombs at Anyang. Development of writing in China.	
Celts move across Europe. 	Arrival of Israelites in Canaan. Philistines settle in Palestine. Israelites ruled by **King David**, then **King Solomon**. Their kingdom split into Israel and Judah. The Phoenicians prosper. Destruction of Jerusalem by Babylonians, and people taken into captivity. Movement of Scythian horse breeders across Asia. Conquest of Eastern Mediterranean lands by **Alexander the Great** Conquest by Romans.	Vedas (religious writings). Birth of **Gautama (the Buddha)**. **Alexander the Great's** campaigns in India. 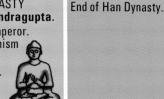	CHOU DYNASTIES. Birth of **Confucius**.  Period of warring states. Unification of China under **Shih Huang Ti.** Great Wall built. CH'IN DYNASTY. HAN DYNASTY. Paper invented. Silk Road in use.	The Olmecs in Mexico. Rise of the Maya. 
Conquest of much of North Europe by Romans. 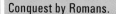 Area becomes part of Roman empire. Barbarians attack Roman empire.  Barbarian kingdoms set up in Britain, France and Germany.	Birth of **Jesus Christ**. Destruction of Jerusalem by Romans. Area becomes part of Eastern Roman (Byzantine) Empire.	MAURYAN DYNASTY founded by **Chandragupta**. **Ashoka** was emperor. Spread of Buddhism through India. GUPTA EMPIRE.	End of Han Dynasty.	Temples at Teotihuacan built.

New Kings in Persia

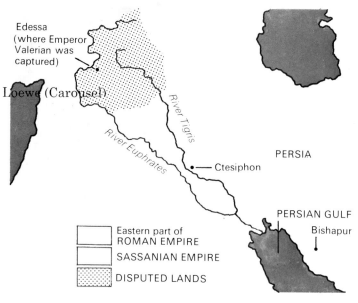

Persia was conquered in 331BC by the Greeks, led by Alexander the Great. After he died, a tribe called the Parthians took over the area and made their capital at Ctesiphon. Their warrior horsemen, shown here, were a continual threat to the Romans in the west.

In AD224, the Parthian king was overthrown by a new leader, who started the Sassanian line of kings. These kings lived and ruled in the style of the great Persian kings of the past. They had pictures of themselves carved in the rocks and worshipped the old Persian god, Ahuramazda. This carving shows Ardashir, the first Sassanian king.

The Sassanian kings built up a large empire. On their western frontier there was endless fighting with the Romans, and some land was claimed by both sides. Shapur I scored a great victory over the Romans in AD260, when he captured their emperor, Valerian. This carving shows the capture.

All trade between East and West had to go through Persia, so it became very wealthy. Shapur I had a grand new palace built at Bishapur. We have some idea of what life was like there from scenes carved on

silver bowls which have been dug up. This picture shows a banquet at the palace. The Sassanian empire finally collapsed in AD637 when the Muslim Arabs invaded.

How Christianity Survived

Barbarian invaders overran most of Western Europe in the 5th century, but Ireland escaped. Groups of monks lived there in small settlements, like this, dedicating their lives to God.

These Irish monks produced some beautiful books, written and decorated completely by hand. This is a page from the Book of Durrow.

Some monks set off from Ireland in tiny open boats to convert the heathens. One of the most famous is St Columba, who founded a settlement on the Island of Iona, off the west coast of Scotland.

The few Christians who remained in other parts of Western Europe also tried to convert people. One of the stories from this time tells of St Coifi, who lived in the north of England. He wanted to show the heathens how powerless their gods were, so he rode into one of their holy places and hurled his spear at the statues there. When the heathens saw that nothing dreadful happened, many decided that he was right and became Christians.

The Beginning of a New Religion

Soon after AD600,* in the land of Arabia, a man called Muhammad was preaching a new religion. He believed in Allah, the "One God". By the time of his death, most people in Arabia followed his religion and called him the Prophet.

In Europe, most people in the Roman Empire were Christians. But when the Empire was invaded, many of them began worshipping other gods. The eastern part of the Roman Empire (called the Byzantine Empire) was not invaded and stayed Christian.

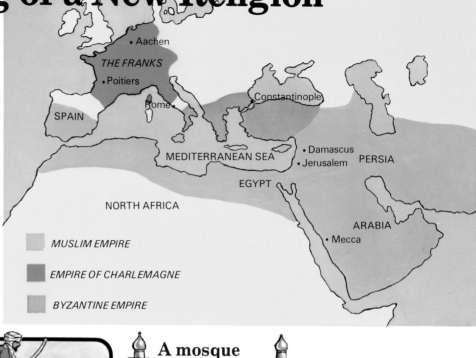

- THE FRANKS
- Aachen
- Poitiers
- Rome
- SPAIN
- Constantinople
- MEDITERRANEAN SEA
- Damascus
- Jerusalem
- PERSIA
- EGYPT
- NORTH AFRICA
- ARABIA
- Mecca

MUSLIM EMPIRE

EMPIRE OF CHARLEMAGNE

BYZANTINE EMPIRE

1 Islam — Page from Koran.

The teachings of Muhammad were collected and written down in a book called the Koran. His faith became known as Islam and his followers were called Muslims.

2

The caliphs, who were Muhammad's successors, believed that everyone should become Muslims. They fought many wars to spread their faith and conquered a great empire.

3

These Muslims are making a pilgrimage to Mecca, the home of Muhammad. All Muslims are meant to visit Mecca at least once in their lives.

4

Muslims eat and drink only at night during the month they call Ramadan. Good Muslims also give money to the poor.

A mosque

Tower called a minaret. People are called to prayer from here by a man called a muezzin.

Recess, called the Mihrab, which shows the direction of Mecca.

Fountain where people must wash before praying.

Muslims should pray five times every day, facing towards Mecca. On Fridays, prayers are said in buildings, like this, called mosques.

*AD stands for two Latin words. Dates with AD next to them are that number of years after the birth of Christ.

Christians in Europe

1 The Christian Church in western Europe was led by the Pope, seen here with one of his priests. Many popes sent out missionaries to persuade people to become Christians.

2 Some missionaries were killed by the people they tried to convert. It was several hundred years before people in Europe accepted Christianity as their religion.

3 The Muslims began to invade southern Europe. In AD732, Charles Martel, king of a people called the Franks, stopped their advance by defeating them at the Battle of Poitiers.

4 This is Roderigo of Bivar, who was known as El Cid, which means "The Lord". He helped to keep the Muslims out of northern Spain and became a great Christian hero.

5 In AD768, Charlemagne (Charles the Great) became King of the Franks. He conquered a lot of Europe and became its first great leader since the fall of the Roman Empire.

6 Charlemagne forced the people he conquered to become Christians, and fought the Muslims in Spain. On Christmas Day AD800, Pope Leo III crowned him Holy Roman Emperor.

7 This gold image of Charlemagne was made to put his skull in.

After Charlemagne's death his empire was divided. The Holy Roman Emperors ruled only the German-speaking peoples of Europe from then on, but were still very powerful.

8 Emperors and popes often quarrelled over power. After one quarrel, Pope Gregory VII kept Henry IV waiting in the snow outside Canossa Castle for three days before he would forgive him. Quarrels between other emperors and popes resulted in long, bitter wars in Germany and Italy.

Key dates

AD570/632	Life of **Muhammad.**
AD622	First year of the Muslim calendar.
AD630	Mecca surrendered to Muhammad.
AD635	Muslims captured Damascus.
AD637/642	Muslims conquered Persia.
AD638	Muslims captured Jerusalem.
AD641/642	Muslims conquered Egypt.
By AD700	All North Africa conquered by Muslims.
AD732	Battle of Poitiers.
AD768/814	Reign of **Charlemagne.**
AD800	**Charlemagne** crowned Holy Roman Emperor.
AD1077	Meeting at Canossa between **Henry IV** and **Gregory VII.**
AD1043/1099	Life of **El Cid.**

Life in Viking Times

In Denmark, Norway and Sweden there lived a people called the North or Norsemen. They were farmers, fishermen and traders. Norsemen who sailed abroad were called Vikings. Some Vikings settled in France and became known as Normans.

Burial mounds

Wooden rampart

Wooden houses

Wooden cart

Chief's hall

Fishermen returning home.

A few animals spend the winter in their owner's house. The rest were killed in the autumn and the meat salted to make it keep.

Carving a walrus tusk.

Sledge

Bed

Wooden bucket

Vikings lived in settlements like this one. The wall and part of the roof of the chief's house have been cut away so that you can see inside.

Carvings

The Vikings were skilled wood-carvers and metal-workers. This carved wooden head is from a wagon.

Runes

Memorial stones to the dead were sometimes set up. These usually had letters called runes carved on them.

A burial

This is the grave of a Viking warrior. Later it will be covered with earth. His possessions, including his animals and sometimes even a slave, were buried with him. The Vikings believed that dead warriors went to "Valhalla", the hall of the gods.

Viking raiders

The men row when they are setting off and landing and when there is not enough wind for sailing.

When they are out of sight of land they steer by the Pole Star and the sun.

Steering oar

Ropes at bottom corners turn sail to catch the wind.

The Vikings were sailors, warriors and adventurers. At first they robbed and plundered other lands. Later they settled in many parts of Europe, including Iceland.

From Iceland they went to Greenland and from there they are thought to have reached America. Long poems, called sagas, were written about brave Viking heroes.

The Vikings in France (Normans) were great soldiers. In AD1066, William, Duke of Normandy conquered England. Another group set out and conquered Sicily and part of Italy.

Where the Vikings went

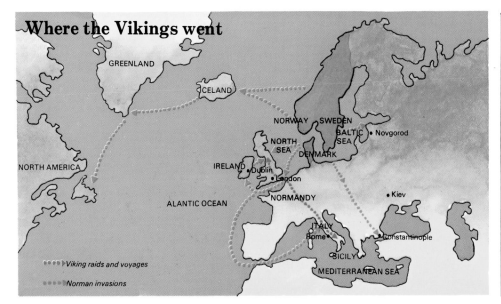

GREENLAND

ICELAND

NORWAY SWEDEN

NORTH SEA

BALTIC SEA • Novgorod

DENMARK

IRELAND • Dublin • London

NORTH AMERICA

ALANTIC OCEAN

NORMANDY

• Kiev

ITALY
Rome •

• Constantinople

SICILY

MEDITERRANEAN SEA

Viking raids and voyages

Norman invasions

Key dates

AD793/900 Great Viking raids on British Isles and northern France.

AD862 Viking settlers in Kiev and Novgorod in Russia.

AD870/930 Iceland colonized by Vikings.

AD900/911 Normandy settled by Vikings.

AD960 **Harald Bluetooth,** King of Denmark, converted to Christianity.

AD1000 Vikings reached America.

AD1016 **Knut** became King of England.

AD1066 **William of Normandy** (William the Conqueror), descendant of Viking settlers, conquered England. Other Normans conquered part of Italy.

Kings, Knights and Castles

All the countries of Europe were organized in roughly the same way in the Middle Ages. A king or emperor ruled a whole country and owned all the land.

The king sometimes needed support or money for a particular plan. So he called a meeting of his nobles, bishops and specially chosen knights and townsmen to discuss it with him. This was the beginning of parliaments.

The king divided his land amongst his most important men. In return, they did "homage" to him. This meant that they knelt in front of him and promised to serve him and fight for him, whenever they were needed. These men were the nobles.

Each noble divided his land among knights who did homage to him. Peasants served a noble or knight and, in return, were allowed to live on his land. This arrangement of exchanging land for services is called the "feudal system".

Castles were uncomfortable places to live. They were damp, cold and draughty. Early castles had no glass in the windows and there was no running water. They were lit by torches made of twigs or rushes.

Kings and nobles built castles to protect themselves against enemies. These might be foreign invaders, other nobles or even rebellious peasants. We have taken away two walls so you can see inside.

Travelling bringing gu

Archers practising

Stables

Armour makers

Becoming a knight

A boy who wanted to be a knight was sent to a noble's house as a page. He was taught to fight and to behave properly.

When he was older he became a squire. It was his job to serve a knight and to follow him into battle. Here is a squire with his knight.

If he proved himself to be worthy of the honour, a noble, perhaps even the king, would "knight" the young man.

The new knight's father or another noble usually gave him some land with peasants and villages. This was called a manor.

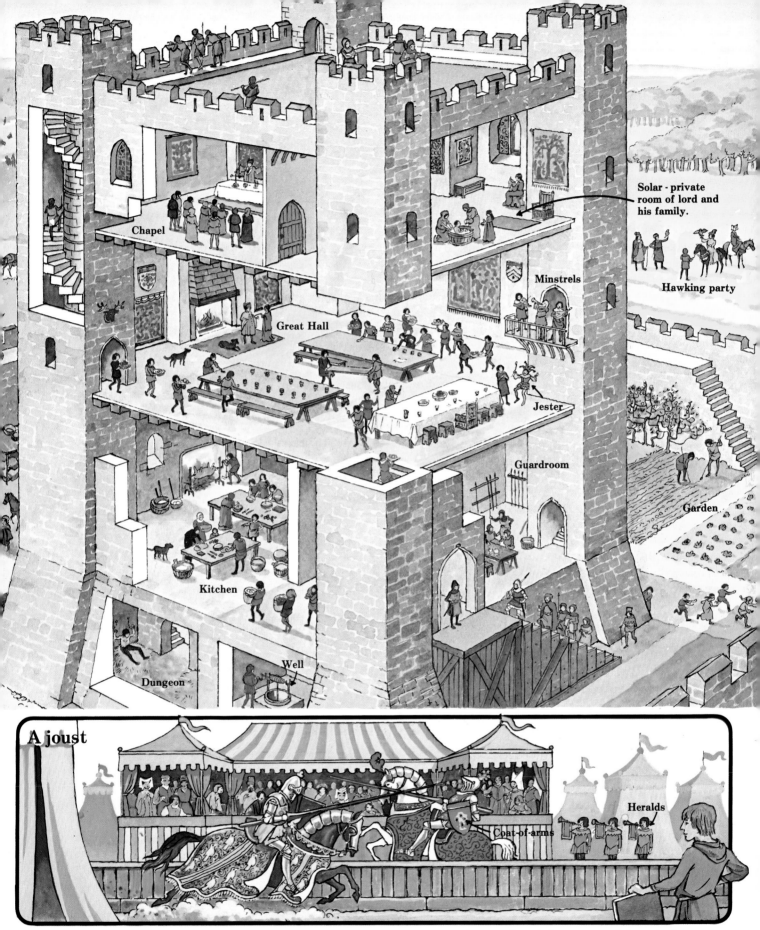

Chapel

Solar - private
room of lord and
his family.

Hawking party

Great Hall

Minstrels

Jester

Guardroom

Garden

Kitchen

Well

Dungeon

A joust

Coat-of-arms

Heralds

To keep in practice for battle, knights took part in specially organized fights. These were called tournaments or jousts. At a joust, two knights on horseback charged at each other with long lances, and tried to knock each other to the ground. Each noble family had a "coat-of-arms", which was painted on their shields, so they could be recognized in armour.

A knight wore a ribbon, badge or scarf belonging to his favourite lady. This was called her "favour". If he won he brought great honour to her as well as to himself.

Village Life

In the Middle Ages, most people in Europe lived in villages. Each village was controlled by the Lord of the Manor. It usually had three fields, divided into strips, which the lord allowed the villagers to farm. They paid him by working for him and by giving him some of the food they grew.

All the peasants can use the common. They can graze their animals here and gather wood and berries.

The ford is a shallow part of the stream, where people can cross.

Fisherman. The Church said people should always eat fish on Fridays.

Ford

The villagers are holding a fair. This is their only chance to buy goods from outside the village. Jugglers, acrobats and musicians have come to perform at the fair.

Priest's house

Dancing bear

Merchants are coming to the fair to buy the villagers' wool.

Black death

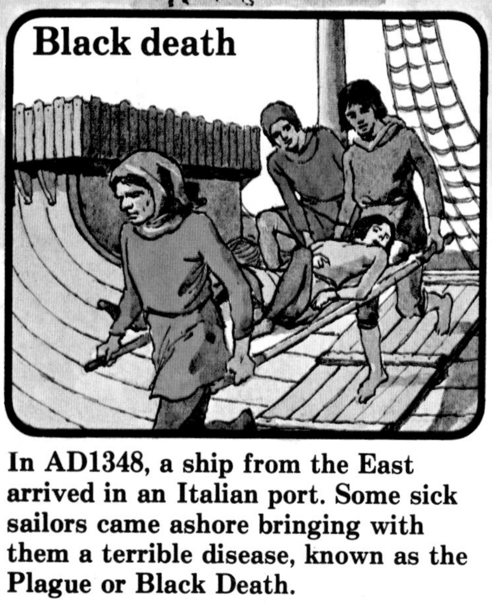

In AD1348, a ship from the East arrived in an Italian port. Some sick sailors came ashore bringing with them a terrible disease, known as the Plague or Black Death.

The Plague quickly spread across Europe because people knew little about medicine or the need to be clean. About one person in every three died from it.

Villagers harvesting wheat. Next year they will grow barley here.

The Lord of the Manor lives here in the Manor House.

Lord of the Manor going hunting. The peasants are forbidden to kill any game animals because that would spoil the lord's hunting.

Stray animals are put in a "pound" and their owners have to pay a fine before they can get them out.

Everyone has their grain ground into flour at the village mill.

In this field barley is growing. Next year it will be left unplanted.

Hole for smoke to come out.

Ale house

Blacksmith

Stocks

Roof made of straw or reeds. This is called thatch.

Vegetable plot and garden

Spinning wool

This field has been left fallow (unplanted) this year. This will make it more fertile for wheat next year.

Tinker coming to fair to mend and sell metal pots and pans.

Towns and Trade

This is what towns looked like in the Middle Ages. The streets were made of earth or cobbles and were narrow and dirty. There were no underground drains so people threw their rubbish into the street. Rich merchants built their houses of stone but most houses were made of wood, so fire was always a great danger. Towns were very small by modern standards and were surrounded by high stone walls.

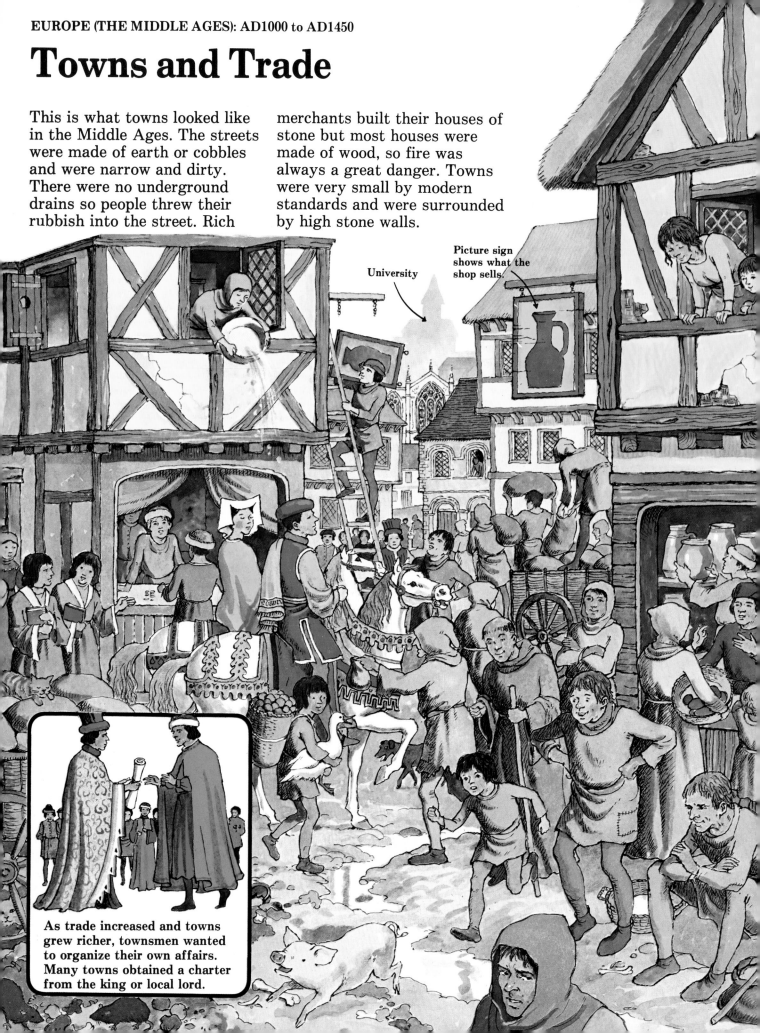

University

Picture sign shows what the shop sells.

As trade increased and towns grew richer, townsmen wanted to organize their own affairs. Many towns obtained a charter from the king or local lord.

1 Guilds

Each trade and craft had its own guild. The guild organized its members by fixing prices and standards of workmanship.

2

A boy who wanted to learn a trade was "apprenticed" to a master. He lived in his master's house and worked in his shop.

3

After seven years he made a special piece of work called a masterpiece. If it was good enough he could join the guild.

4

The mayor and corporation, who ran the city, were chosen from the most important members of each of the guilds.

5

When the population increased men could not find places as guild members so they had to work for others for wages.

Mystery plays

On special holidays each guild acted different scenes from the Bible. These were called "mystery" plays. The guilds acted their plays on wagons called pageants, which they moved around the town between each performance. Many people could not read so the plays helped them to get to know the stories in the Bible. In many towns the guild which did the best play won a prize.

1 Trade

Banker

The first bankers were rich merchants who lent money to people wanting to organize trading expeditions.

2

Spices, jewels and silks were brought to Europe from India and China. Italian merchants controlled this trade.

3

Goods were carried overland by packhorses. Most roads were very bad and there were often bandits in lonely areas.

4

Sea travel was also difficult and dangerous. Sailors steered by the stars and tried to keep close to the land whenever they could.

The Church

1 The head of the Church in western Europe, the Pope, was elected by cardinals (the highest rank of priests) at a meeting called a conclave.

At one time there were three rival popes who all claimed to have been elected by a conclave. This argument was called the Great Schism.

2 Everyone went to church. All the services were in Latin, although only the priests and highly-educated people understood it.

3 Few people could read and write, except priests, so kings used priests as secretaries and advisers. Priests of high rank were summoned to parliament.

4 No one in Europe had discovered how to print books. All books were written by hand by monks and were often decorated with bright colours and gold leaf.

5 People who refused to believe everything that the Church taught were called heretics and were sometimes burnt to death. Joan of Arc was burnt as a heretic but later people decided she was a saint.

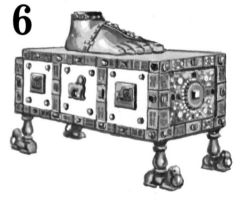

6 Bodies of saints or holy objects were often put into jewelled containers called reliquaries. These were treated with great respect and people worshipped in front of them.

Pilgrims

Some people went on journeys to holy places to show their devotion to God, to be forgiven for some sin or cured of an illness. These journeys were called pilgrimages.

Life in a nunnery

Some people chose to give their lives completely to God's service and to live apart from the rest of the world. Women who did this were called nuns and lived in nunneries. Men were called monks and lived in monasteries. Trainee monks and nuns were called novices.

Nuns are always ready to give food and beds to tired pilgrims and travellers.

Abbess's house

Peasants from the village working on nunnery lands.

Nun giving food to some poor people

Stables

Visitors' houses

Cloisters where nuns take exercise.

Chapter House where meetings are held.

Dormitory

Refectory, where the nuns eat their meals. In some nunneries they eat in silence while a religious book is read to them.

Hospice where nuns look after people who are ill.

Nuns and monks promised to obey their superiors, to give up everything they owned and never to marry. Each day was divided into special times for prayer, study and work.

Like any Lord of the Manor, a nunnery had land. Rich people often left land and money to the nuns when they died, so that the nuns would pray for them. Some nunneries became extremely rich.

Key dates

AD1181/1226 Life of **St Francis of Assisi.**
AD1100s and 1200s Quarrels between popes and emperors led to wars in Germany and Italy.
AD1265/1321 The poet **Dante** lived.
AD1273 **Rudolf of Habsburg** became King of the Germans. His family ruled until 1918.
AD1307/1314 The Knights Templar were disbanded.
AD1337/1453 The "Hundred Years" War between England and France.
AD1370/1417 The Great Schism.
AD1380/1422 Quarrels between French nobles helped the English in the war.
AD1412/1431 Life of **Joan of Arc.** She led the French to victory in the war but was then burnt as a heretic.

Wars Between Religions

1 Constantinople

When invaders overran the western part of the Roman Empire, the eastern (Byzantine) half survived. The city of Constantinople was its capital.

2

These are priests of the Byzantine "Orthodox" Church. Over the years, eastern Christians developed slightly different beliefs from those of the west.

3

Between AD632 and 645 Muslims conquered part of the Byzantine Empire. Here their caliph (ruler) enters Jerusalem. Later, emperors and caliphs made peace.

4

Many Christian pilgrims visited the Holy Land, where Jesus had lived. The Muslims allowed them to continue these visits.

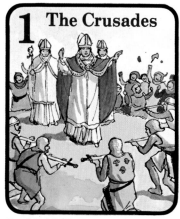

1 The Crusades

In AD1095, Pope Urban II gave a sermon at Clermont in France. He inspired his listeners to go on a crusade (holy war).

2

The Crusaders set out on the long and difficult journey to the Holy Land to win it back from the Muslims.

The leaders of the First Crusade were French noblemen but their followers came from many different countries.

3

The Crusaders arrived in Constantinople and met the Emperor. At first he was friendly but really he did not trust them.

7 Saladin

The Muslims, under a great leader called Saladin, won back Jerusalem from the quarrelling Christians. Several new crusades set out from Europe to try to win it back.

8

The feeling between the Byzantines and the European Crusaders became so bad that one group of Crusaders attacked Constantinople itself and set up their own emperor.

9 Richard the Lionheart

Richard the Lionheart of England, Frederick II of Germany and St Louis of France tried to save Outremer but by AD1291 the Muslims had recaptured the Holy Land.

5 In the 11th century*, Seljuk Turks, who were also Muslims, arrived in the area from the east. They were very unfriendly to the Christians.

6 When the Turks defeated the Byzantines at the Battle of Manzikert, the western Christians felt they must go and fight to protect the Holy Land.

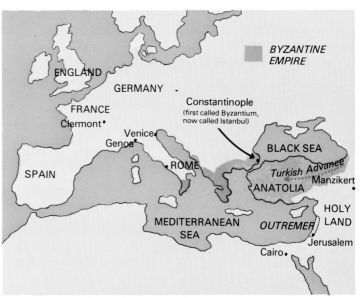

BYZANTINE EMPIRE

ENGLAND
GERMANY
FRANCE
Clermont•
Venice
Genoa
SPAIN
ROME
Constantinople (first called Byzantium, now called Istanbul)
BLACK SEA
Turkish Advance
Manzikert
ANATOLIA
MEDITERRANEAN SEA
OUTREMER
HOLY LAND
Jerusalem
Cairo•

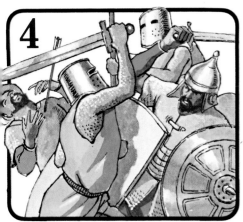

4 The Crusaders left Constantinople and went to fight the Muslims. They were very successful. The Holy Land became a Christian kingdom, called Outremer.

Knight Templar
Knight Hospitaller
Teutonic Knight

5 Special groups of soldier-monks were formed to care for pilgrims and to fight the Muslims. One knight from each of the three most important groups is shown here.

6 Some Crusaders settled in Outremer. When new Crusaders came out they were shocked to find the settlers quarrelling with each other but making friends with Muslim rulers.

10 The Byzantines won back Constantinople but the days of their wealth and power were over. In AD1453, with the help of cannons, the Turks finally captured the city.

How to spot a Crusader's tomb

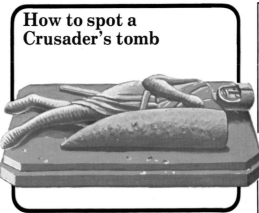

Here is the tomb of a knight. His crossed legs show that he was a Crusader. Look out for a tomb like this if you go inside a church.

Key dates

AD632/645	Muslims seized parts of Byzantine Empire.
AD638	Caliph Omar took Jerusalem.
AD1000/1100	Turks invaded Byzantine Empire.
AD1071	Battle of Manzikert.
AD1095	Sermon at Clermont.
AD1096	First Crusade. Jerusalem taken. Outremer founded.
AD1187	**Saladin** took Jerusalem.
AD1191	Crusade of **Richard the Lionheart.**
AD1204	Sack of Constantinople.
AD1228/1244	**Emperor Frederick II** won back Jerusalem for a while.
AD1249/1270	Crusades of **St Louis**
AD1261	Byzantine Emperor recaptured Constantinople.
AD1291	The end of Outremer.
AD1453	Turks captured Constantinople. (End of Byzantine Empire.)

This means the 100 years between AD1000 and AD1100.

How Muslim People Lived

The Arabs were the first Muslims and they conquered a huge empire. At first the whole Muslim empire was ruled by one caliph, but later it split into several kingdoms. Life for the Muslims was often more advanced than life in Europe. After they had conquered the eastern provinces of the Roman Empire, they absorbed many of the ideas of ancient Greece and Rome. Trading made them wealthy, and this brought more comfort and luxury into their lives.

Arab nomads

Many Arabs were nomads, who moved with their animals in search of water and pasture. They did not change their way of life even after they conquered their huge empire.

Peasants in Muslim lands went on working their fields. Much of the land was hot and dry and they had to work hard to keep it watered.

Muslim cities

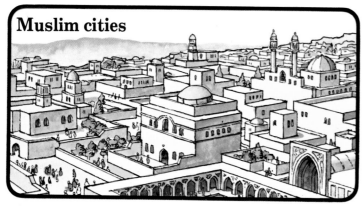

Houses in Muslim cities were often covered with white plaster, which helped to keep them cool. They faced inwards on to open courtyards, which provided shade. The streets were usually narrow and there were few open spaces except around the mosques.

Market

Towns usually had a souq (market). The streets where it was held were often roofed over. Shops in one street usually sold the same kind of goods.

Baths

Palaces and many private houses had baths and there were also public baths. They were copied from the designs of Roman baths.

1 Learning

Arabic writing

Arabic numbers

Our numbers

The Muslims developed a way of writing which read from right to left. Their system of numbers was simpler than the Roman figures used in Europe.

Arab astronomers

Muslim scholars studied Greek and Roman learning. They were especially interested in mathematics, the stars, geography, law, religion and medicine.

The Arabs made complicated instruments, like this one, which measured the position of ships at sea, by looking at the stars. This instrument is called an astrolabe.

Hospital

Muslim doctors followed ancient Greek methods of treating the sick. Hospitals were built to care for people who needed special treatment.

Harem windows

3 Muslim rulers built themselves huge palaces, like this one. These were beautifully decorated by skilled craftsmen, and were very comfortable, compared with European castles built at this time. They usually had gardens set out in patterns around fountains. Life in these palaces was very formal, with lots of ceremonies.

4 Part of a house was set aside for women only. This was called the harem. No man from outside the family could enter it. In the street, Muslim women wore veils.

Arab traders

Arab dhow

Trading played an important part in Muslim life. Arabs travelled to many different countries to find new customers. By sea they travelled in fast ships, called dhows. Some Arabs still use dhows today.

On land, merchants travelled by camel in groups called caravans. On main routes, caravansarays (shelters) were built at a day's journey from each other. Travellers could spend the night there.

Muslim art

Close-up of tiles

Tiles

Carpet

Incense burner

Their religion did not allow Muslim artists to make sculptures of the human figure. They used patterns, flowers, animals and birds as decoration. Tiles were often used for decorating buildings.

Muslim craftsmen were famous for the manufacture of beautiful carpets and for their metal work. The bronze lion, shown above, was used for holding burning incense. Crusaders who returned to the west took treasures like these back with them. The work of Muslim craftsmen became popular in Europe.

Genghis Khan and his Empire

The Mongols were nomads who wandered across the plains of Asia with their herds of horses. From AD1206, a chief called Temujin overpowered all the Mongol tribes and conquered a huge empire. He became known as Ghengis Khan, the Great Prince. His sons raided Europe and his grandson, Kubilai Khan, conquered China. The Mongols were then weakened by family quarrels and fierce resistance. Later, a chief called Tamerlane* conquered an empire of his own and invaded India.

Muslim city being destroyed by Mongol raiders.

Mongols fought on horseback, using lances or bows and arrows.

Mongol commander. The Mongol army was very well-disciplined and could travel vast distances very quickly.

Here the Mongols are moving off after destroying an enemy city. The Mongols were very cruel to their enemies. Millions of people were killed or made slaves.

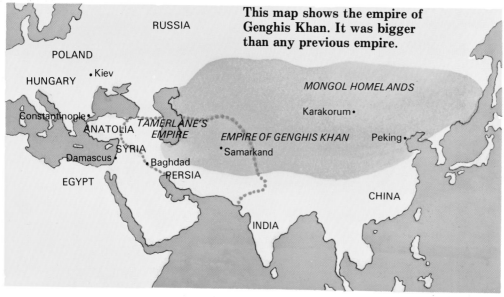

This map shows the empire of Genghis Khan. It was bigger than any previous empire.

RUSSIA
POLAND
HUNGARY
Kiev
Constantinople
ANATOLIA
TAMERLANE'S EMPIRE
SYRIA
Damascus
Baghdad
PERSIA
EGYPT
EMPIRE OF GENGHIS KHAN
Samarkand
MONGOL HOMELANDS
Karakorum
Peking
CHINA
INDIA

A friar visits the Mongols

A Christian friar, called William of Rubruck, was sent by St Louis of France to visit the Mongols. The Mongols had their own gods, but several of their

Tamerlane is sometimes known as Tamburlaine.

Slaves

The yurts (tents) are packed up and put on horses.

Chief's tent being carried by ox-drawn cart.

Genghis Khan organized his empire very efficiently. He drew up a clear law code called the Yasa, encouraged trade, punished bandits and started a messenger service.

Some Mongols settled in the newly conquered lands and built cities. Others continued to live as nomads in tents. There are Mongols who still live this way today.

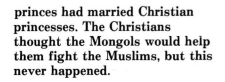

princes had married Christian princesses. The Christians thought the Mongols would help them fight the Muslims, but this never happened.

1 Tamerlane

This is the Mongol chief Timur the Lame, known in Europe as Tamerlane. He ruled his empire from the city of Samarkand.

2

This is the building in Samarkand where Tamerlane was buried. Russian archaeologists have opened his tomb.

3

By using modern methods scientists built up a face on his skull, so that we now know what he looked like.

115

Princes and Temples

1 India was divided into kingdoms ruled by wealthy princes. They built themselves luxurious palaces and kept musicians and dancers to entertain them.

2 Indian villagers worked hard to keep their fields watered for growing rice. Each village was run by a headman who carried out the orders of the local ruler.

3 Indians did most of their trade with Arabs. They sold silks, ivory, pearls, spices and perfumes and bought Arab horses, which were especially beautiful and could run fast.

4 Many people, both inside and outside India, had accepted the teachings of the Buddha. Pilgrims, like this Chinese monk, travelled a long way to visit sacred Buddhist shrines.

5 The ancient Hindu faith became popular again. There were many gods and goddesses but the god Shiva, shown above, was one of the most important ones.

6 Hindus believe that all rivers come from the gods. The river Ganges, shown above, is especially holy. For thousands of years they have bathed in it to wash away their sins.

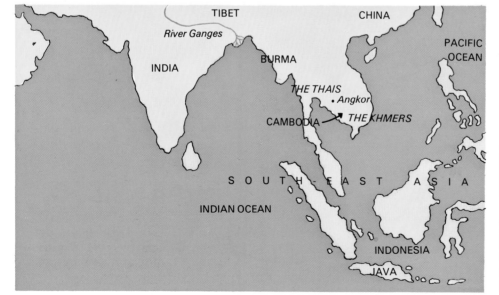

Indian ideas in other countries

Indian religions, ideas and ways of life spread to other countries, especially in South-East Asia. This is a Buddhist temple at Borobudur on the island of Java in Indonesia.

Angkor

One of the countries that was influenced by Indian ideas was Cambodia. In the ninth century a people called the Khmers rose to power there. They worshipped their own kings as gods on earth, but they also worshipped Hindu gods and built huge temples, like this one at Angkor. In AD1431 a people called the Thais invaded Cambodia. The great cities and temples of the Khmers were abandoned and the jungle grew up and covered them.

In AD1296 a Chinese visitor to Cambodia saw a procession like this and wrote an account of it.

How we know

Pictures, like this, were cut into the stone of Angkor. They tell us about the battles, on land and rivers, fought by the Khmers against their enemies the Chams and Thais.

The stone carvings at Angkor also tell us about the everyday life of the Khmers. This picture shows two men and their friends getting ready to watch a fight between two cockerels.

Silk and Spice Traders

In AD589 a new dynasty (family line) of emperors, called the Sui, began to rule China. They brought peace to the country after a time of long and difficult wars between rival Chinese groups.

Civil servants helped the Emperor to rule. They had to take exams before they were given jobs in government. In the countryside, the nobles, who owned most of the land, gradually became more powerful.

Buddhism had spread from India in the first century AD and was very popular. But many people still believed in the teachings of Confucius and the Taoist religion. At times Buddhists were persecuted.

A trading city in China

Some merchants travelled by sea to Africa and the Middle East.

Chinese inventions

The Chinese were the inventors of several things that were unknown to the rest of the world at this time.

They discovered how to make porcelain, a very hard, fine type of china.

At this time, the Chinese were using compasses to find their way across land and sea. This one is made of lacquered wood.

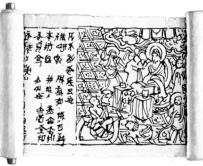

By the 10th century they were using wooden blocks to print books. This is probably the oldest printed page in the world.

Gunpowder was first used for fireworks. By the 13th century the Chinese were also using it for bombs and other weapons.

118

2

Chinese craftsmen were very skilful. At the time when the T'ang family were emperors (AD618/906) they made especially fine pottery figures of animals and servants. These were placed in tombs.

3

In AD1279 the Mongols, led by the great Kubilai Khan, overran China, which they then ruled for nearly 100 years.

Key dates

AD589/618	Sui Dynasty ruled.
AD618/906	T'ang Dynasty ruled. Buddhism very popular.
AD960/1279	Sung Dynasty ruled. Growth of trade. Mongols started attacking northern frontier.
AD1279/1368	Mongols ruled China.
AD1276/1292	**Marco Polo's** trip to China.
AD1368	Mongol rulers overthrown.
AD1368/1644	Ming Dynasty ruled.

Silk, porcelain (fine china) and carved jade were taken to the west and traded for silver and gold. Many cities grew rich because of this trade.

This caravan of camels is setting out with goods destined for the Middle East and Europe.

1 Marco Polo

Many foreign merchants, especially Arabs, came to China to trade. Later, a few adventurous Europeans arrived. Two of the European merchants who visited China were the brothers, Nicolo and Maffeo Polo, from Venice. On their second visit they took Nicolo's young son, Marco. Here they are meeting Kubilai Khan, the Mongol emperor of China.

2

Marco Polo travelled around Kubilai Khan's empire for nearly 17 years. When he returned home, he wrote a book about his travels. This is the first page of his book.

Land of the Samurai

Japan is a group of islands off the coast of China. We know little about its early history because the Japanese had no writing until it was introduced from China in the fifth century AD. The Buddhist religion also came from China and won many followers, although Japan's ancient religion, Shinto, was still popular. Japanese arts, crafts, laws, taxes and the organization of government were also based on Chinese ideas.

SEA OF JAPAN

JAPAN

• Heian (now Kyoto)

PACIFIC OCEAN

1 This is part of the Imperial city, Heian, later called Kyoto. The emperor was at the centre of power, but noble clans (families) gradually took over and ruled for him. Many emperors retired to Buddhist monasteries. As "Cloistered Ex-Emperors", some re-established their power for a time.

2 Legally all the land in Japan was owned by the emperor. He allowed farmers, like these, to use it in return for taxes and services. Later, the nobles began to acquire their own private lands because the Emperor was not strong enough to stop them. Many battles were fought about the possession of land and nobles gave it to their supporters as rewards.

3 This is Yoritomo, military leader and the chief of the Minamoto clan. In AD1192 he began to use the title "Shogun". This became the name for the head of government and was passed from father to son.

Poetry

Poetry was popular, especially among the people at court. People made trips to look at the cherry blossom and see the maple leaves turning red. This inspired them to recite and write poems. There were several famous women poets.

Novels

The Japanese liked novels. This is Murasaki Shikibu, a court lady, who wrote a famous novel called *The Tale of Genji*.

Armour making

Japanese warriors wore suits of armour made of tough leather strips. This is an armourer's shop where the suits were made.

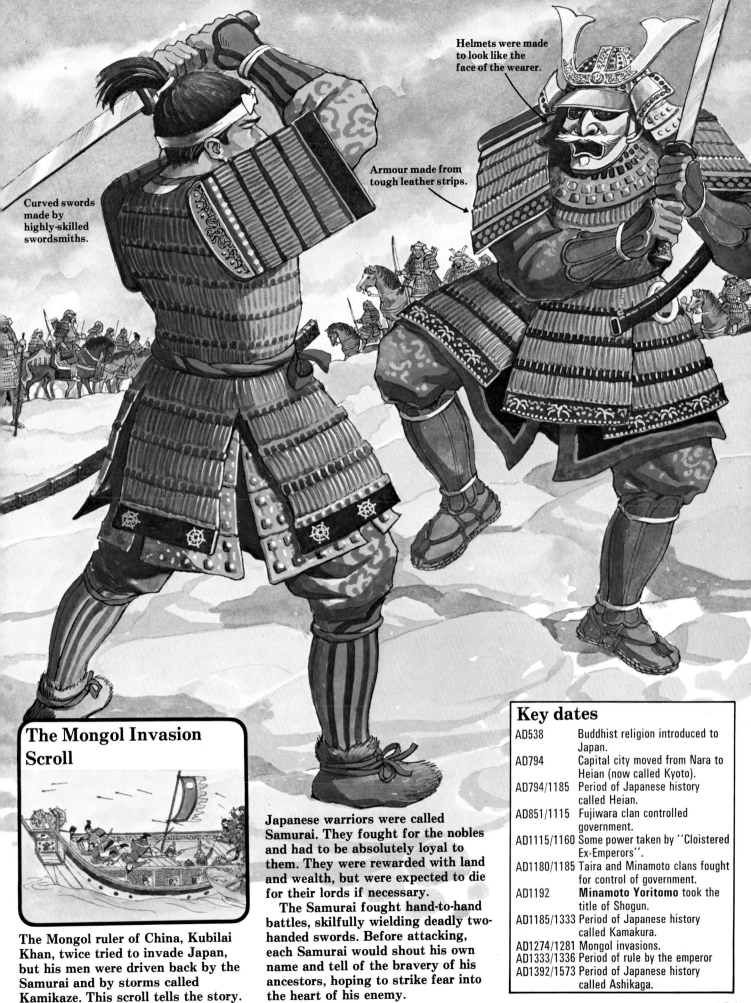

Helmets were made to look like the face of the wearer.

Armour made from tough leather strips.

Curved swords made by highly-skilled swordsmiths.

The Mongol Invasion Scroll

The Mongol ruler of China, Kubilai Khan, twice tried to invade Japan, but his men were driven back by the Samurai and by storms called Kamikaze. This scroll tells the story.

Japanese warriors were called Samurai. They fought for the nobles and had to be absolutely loyal to them. They were rewarded with land and wealth, but were expected to die for their lords if necessary.

The Samurai fought hand-to-hand battles, skilfully wielding deadly two-handed swords. Before attacking, each Samurai would shout his own name and tell of the bravery of his ancestors, hoping to strike fear into the heart of his enemy.

Key dates

AD538	Buddhist religion introduced to Japan.
AD794	Capital city moved from Nara to Heian (now called Kyoto).
AD794/1185	Period of Japanese history called Heian.
AD851/1115	Fujiwara clan controlled government.
AD1115/1160	Some power taken by "Cloistered Ex-Emperors".
AD1180/1185	Taira and Minamoto clans fought for control of government.
AD1192	**Minamoto Yoritomo** took the title of Shogun.
AD1185/1333	Period of Japanese history called Kamakura.
AD1274/1281	Mongol invasions.
AD1333/1336	Period of rule by the emperor
AD1392/1573	Period of Japanese history called Ashikaga.

Kingdoms, Traders and Tribes

In AD639, Arabs, inspired by their new religion, Islam, invaded Egypt and then north Africa. They traded with the local people and brought new wealth to the area.

South of the Sahara, the land was often difficult to clear and live in. There were also dangerous diseases there. As people learnt how to make strong tools from iron, tribes were able to progress further south, clearing and farming the land as they went.

1 West African kingdoms

Arab traders began to make regular journeys across the Sahara. They bought gold and salt from West Africa and sold it in busy Mediterranean ports.

MEDITERRANEAN SEA

MOROCCO

THE SAHARA

Timbuktu

KINGDOM OF MALI

A F R I C A

River Niger

River Congo

MUSLIM EMPIRE

ATLANTIC OCEAN

African king

KALAHARI DESERT

2

Trade made the local Africans very rich. They built magnificent cities full of palaces and mosques. The most famous city was Timbuktu shown here.

3

Arab visitors

Some of the West African rulers had large kingdoms. One of the most important was Mali. Several Arabs who travelled to these kingdoms kept records of their visits. They were very impressed by the luxury they found, especially at court. Here, some Arabs are meeting an African king.

Portuguese explorers

From AD1420 onwards, Prince Henry of Portugal, known as "the Navigator", organized expeditions to explore the West African coast and trade with the Africans.

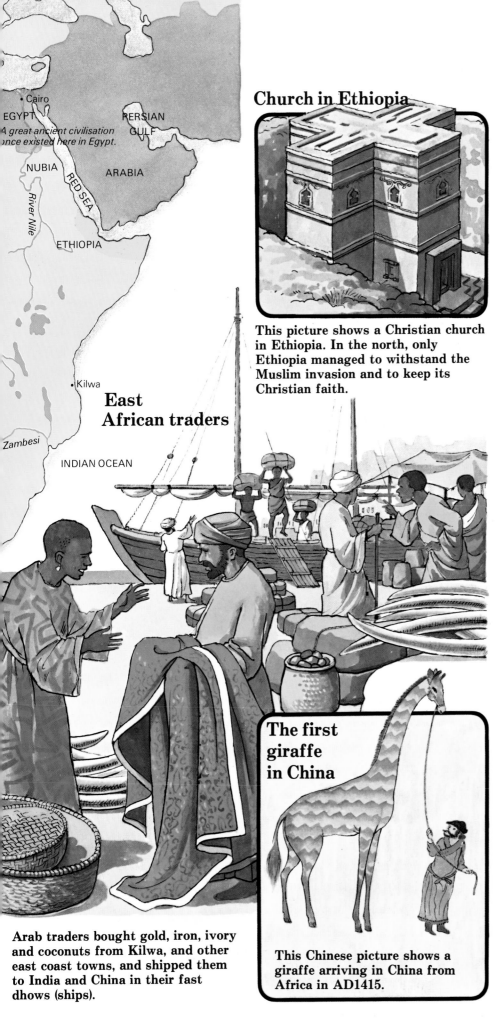

A great ancient civilisation once existed here in Egypt.

East African traders

Arab traders bought gold, iron, ivory and coconuts from Kilwa, and other east coast towns, and shipped them to India and China in their fast dhows (ships).

Church in Ethiopia

This picture shows a Christian church in Ethiopia. In the north, only Ethiopia managed to withstand the Muslim invasion and to keep its Christian faith.

The first giraffe in China

This Chinese picture shows a giraffe arriving in China from Africa in AD1415.

Life in the south

In the south different tribes adopted different ways of life.

1

In the Kalahari Desert the Bushmen hunted animals for their food.

2

Pygmies lived in tropical jungles, hunting animals and gathering berries and fruits.

3

Tribes living in the open plains of the east and south kept animals and farmed the land.

4

People who knew how to make iron tools were very useful to their tribes.

123

Life in North and South America

At this time there were many separate groups of people living in different parts of the huge continent of America. In the forests, mountains, plains, deserts and jungles and in the frozen north, people found ways of surviving by hunting, fishing, gathering, and later farming. The people of North America did not have a system of writing, but archaeologists have found remains of their settlements, which tell us something about their lives.

Huff•

N O R T H   A M E R I C A

•Cahokia

ATLANTIC OCEAN

TOLTECS   MAYA
Tenochtitlan• •Tula YUCATAN
AZTECS
MEXICO
C E N T R A L
A M E R I C A

PACIFIC OCEAN

S O U T H   A M E R I C A

•Chanchan
PERU
•Cuzco

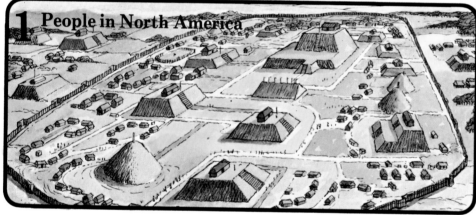

1 People in North America

One of the most advanced groups of North American Indians were the Mississipians or "Mound Builders", who were farmers and traders. In their towns, the temples and other important buildings were built on top of great earth mounds. This picture shows part of Cahokia, one of their towns.

Underground rooms (kivas) were used for religious ceremonies.

Some Indian farmers lived in "pueblos", towns made of stone and mud. The houses were sometimes as high as five floors and were built in canyon walls.

At Huff, on the plains, traces of a village of more than 100 wooden houses, like this, have been found. The village was surrounded by a ditch and palisade (wooden fence).

Eskimos learnt how to live in the intense cold of the far north. They hunted caribou, seals and whales and also fished and trapped birds.

Mountain farmers in Peru

What the Indians made

The people in Peru were skilled potters and metal-workers and expert weavers. Some of the cloth they made has lasted to the present day and is still brightly-coloured. Each of the objects shown above was made by a different people.

The first American farmers we know about lived in the area that is now Peru. They grew maize, vegetables, cotton, tobacco and a drug called coca. Later they built terraces on the mountainside, so that they could grow crops even on the steep slopes of the Andes. Alpacas and llamas provided wool and carried heavy loads.

Towns

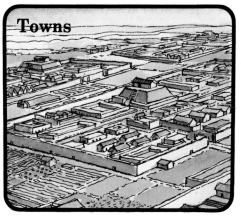

At first, the people of Peru had small settlements. Later they built great monuments and cities, such as the Chimu peoples' capital of Chanchan, shown above.

The Incas

These men are Inca warriors. The Incas were a tribe who lived in the mountains of Peru. The first Inca ruler probably lived about AD1200.

In 1438 a man called Pachacutec became their king and they spread out from the city of Cuzco, their capital, to conquer a huge empire.

Key dates

North America
AD500/1500 The Mound Builders or Mississipians lived.
AD1400/1600 People living at Huff.

South America
AD200/900 Period of Peruvian civilisation called the "Classic Period".
AD1100/1438 Chimu people living at Chanchan.
AD1200 **Manco Capac** ruled the Incas.
AD1438/1471 **Pachacutec** ruled the Incas.

Central America
700BC/AD900 Maya living in Yucatan.
100BC Zapotecs living on the south coast.
AD750/990 The Toltec Empire.
AD1325 Aztecs known to be at Tenochtitlan.

The Aztecs

Aztec numbers

1   20   400   8,000

20+20+20
+20+20=100

Blanket   400

Bag of cocoa

←2

100 bags of cocoa   402 blankets

One of the earliest and greatest peoples of Central America were the Maya. This picture shows a procession of Mayan musicians.

Archaeologists have recently discovered, in the same area, more about a people called the Toltecs. This is a temple in Tula, their capital city.

This is an Aztec warrior. The Aztecs probably came from western Mexico before they settled at Tenochtitlan and conquered all the land around it.

The Aztecs had a system of numbers, which meant they could count and keep record of their possessions. These are some of the symbols they used.

The market place

Dogs, fattened ready to be eaten.

Avocadoes →

Tomatoes

Corn

Limes

Pineapples

Calendar

This picture shows the "New Fire Ceremony", which marked the beginning of a 52 year cycle. There were 18 months in each year.

Schools

Trading between themselves and with people from other towns was an important part of Aztec life. They had no money so they exchanged goods for others of equal value. This is called barter. Chocolate was a favourite drink, so cocoa beans, from which it was made, were always in demand. They were often used for making small payments. Jade and turquoise were more valuable than gold and silver.

Children were taught by their parents. At 15 the boys went to school. Special schools trained boys and girls as priests.

The city of Tenochtitlan

This is the capital city of the Aztecs. It was built on islands in the middle of a lake. The lake no longer exists and modern Mexico City is built on top of it.

The Aztecs worshipped many gods and goddesses. They built temples where they killed human beings and ripped out their hearts, in order to please these gods.

Temple of the Rain God

Human sacrifice

Temple of the War God (Chief Aztec god)

Lake

Temple

Emperor's palace

Temple of the Feathered Serpent, one of the Aztec gods

This wall called the Serpent Wall.

Aztecs playing "tlachtli", a game using a rubber ball.

Special boats collect waste.

Mosaic and feathers

Aztec craftsmen produced beautiful mosaic work, like this mask, which is covered with small pieces of precious turquoise.

Shields, like this one, were made of feathers. The Aztecs also used feathers for making head-dresses and cloaks.

How we know

The Aztecs used a form of picture-writing. It had not developed far enough to record complicated ideas but some religious teachings and history were recorded and have survived in books like the one above. Such a book is called a codex.

127

The Slav People

Many of the people who now live in Eastern Europe and Western Russia are Slavs. They settled in these places in the 700s, after centuries of wandering across Europe. In the west, the Slav people set up several kingdoms for themselves. In the south, they were ruled by a people called Bulgars. In the east, the Slav people settled with the Vikings, who called the area "Rus" and so gave us our name "Russia".

This map shows the Slav kingdoms during the 800s.

Novgorod

KINGDOM OF KIEV

Moscow

THE POLES

KINGDOM OF THE FRANKS

MORAVIA

Kiev

BLACK SEA

KINGDOM OF THE BULGARS

BALTIC SEA

1

Some of the Slav kingdoms became very great and wealthy, but did not last very long. One of these was Moravia. This silver plaque is one of the few Moravian things to have survived.

2

The Southern and Eastern Slavs were converted to Christianity by Byzantine missionaries. This led them to copy the Byzantine art style, as in this picture.

3

The Western Slavs (present-day Poles and Czechs) also became Christians, but they joined the Roman Catholic instead of the Byzantine Church. This is the Polish king, Boleslav I.

4

Some Russian states became wealthy and powerful, and European kings began to take an interest in them. The most important was Kiev. Three of its Grand Prince's daughters married European kings.

5

At the beginning of the 13th century, Russia was invaded by a group of Mongols called Tartars. They destroyed many cities and made others, including the small town of Moscow, shown here, pay them tributes.

6

One Russian prince, called Alexander Nevsky, fought a great battle against the Tartars to save his city, Novgorod. He is still remembered as a great hero.

Kings, Popes and Princes

This picture shows a procession in Florence, the capital city of one of the greatest states in Italy. In the fifteenth century Florence was one of the great banking centres of Europe and was also famous as a clothmaking centre. The ruling family of Florence was called the Medici.

They were very wealthy and spent a lot of money on buying paintings and sculptures and having magnificent buildings constructed, which you can still see if you visit Florence. The most brilliant of the Medici princes was Lorenzo the Magnificent.

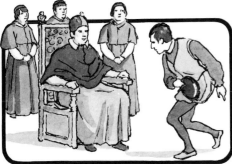

In the 15th century Italy was a collection of separate states. The central area around Rome was ruled by the Pope. Here the Pope is receiving a messenger from a foreign prince.

The Italian states were always fighting each other. In 1494 the French joined the fighting and soon the Spaniards and the emperor of the German states joined in as well.

Venice was one of the wealthiest states in Italy. Its ruler was called the "Doge". This is a portrait of one of the Doges, wearing the special Doge's hat.

Art and Learning

At the end of the 15th century, people in Europe began to take a great interest in art and learning, and to develop new ideas about the world. They started asking questions and doing experiments, instead of just accepting existing ideas.

People began to think that civilisation had been at its best in Ancient Greece and Rome, so they revived Greek and Roman ideas. The time became known as the "Renaissance", which means revival or rebirth. It began in Italy and gradually spread across Europe.

In the Renaissance, Italians began to be interested in the remains of Ancient Rome. They dug up statues and other treasures and made collections of them.

This is the city of Florence in Italy. The new ideas of the Renaissance began here and many of the most famous men of this time lived and worked in Florence.

1 Painting

Before the Renaissance, artists painted mainly religious scenes. Everything in their pictures looked flat and the people did not look very lifelike.

2

In the late 14th and early 15th centuries, painters began to try to make the people in their paintings look as much like living people as possible.

3

Besides painting religious subjects, Renaissance painters did pictures, like this one, of everyday life, and of stories from Ancient Greece and Rome.

Sculpture

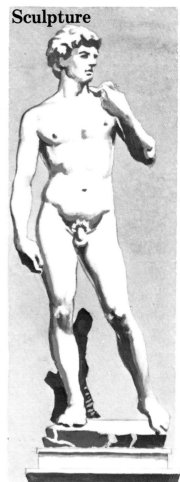

Sculptors were inspired by the statues of Ancient Greece and Rome. This marble statue was made by Michelangelo. He was also a painter, an architect and a poet.

4

For the first time artists began to use live models to help them paint life-like people. This is Simonetta Vespucci, who modelled for the artist Botticelli.

5

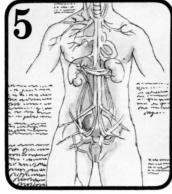

Artists began to study nature and the human body to help them draw things more accurately. This sketch is from the notebook of Leonardo da Vinci.

6

Artists learned how to show distance in their paintings, making you feel you could walk into them. This is called "perspective".

1 Learning

Many new universities and schools were founded. The main subjects were Greek and Latin grammar. In England the new schools were called "grammar" schools.

2

Scholars studied texts in Greek, Latin and Hebrew. They were excited by the thoughts and ideas of ancient times. The invention of printing helped to spread these ideas.

3

Studying ancient Christian texts made some people, like this Dutch scholar called Erasmus, criticize the Church and its priests for being corrupt.

4

People also began to study politics. This is Machiavelli, an Italian who wrote a book about politics called "The Prince", in which he said that a ruler had to be ruthless.

Architecture

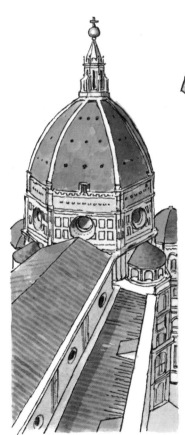

Architects built wonderful palaces and churches. They used domes and copied the style of Greek and Roman temples. The towers and spires of the Middle Ages went out of fashion.

A properly educated Renaissance person was expected to be able to:

understand and collect art, write poetry, play a musical instrument,

read and write Latin and Greek, speak several languages, fight if necessary,

take part in politics, ride and be good at sports, show good manners to everyone.

131

Science and Inventions

1

The new ideas of the Renaissance made people keen to question everything about the world around them. Some people began doing experiments to test their ideas.

2

People called "alchemists", however, tried to brew potions that would cure all ills, give eternal life and turn lead into gold.

3

One of the greatest men of the Renaissance was Leonardo da Vinci. He was a painter and an inventor and he thought a lot about making a flying machine. This is a model based on one of his designs which he worked out by watching birds fly. Leonardo also studied animals and human bodies to find out how they worked and he painted the very famous picture of the Mona Lisa.

4

The printing press was probably the most important invention of this time. The first one was made by a German called Johann Gutenberg. Books could now be produced quickly and cheaply, instead of having to be handwritten as before. This meant ideas and learning spread more quickly.

5

In England, people experimented with metals and learnt how to make cheap and reliable cannons out of cast-iron. These soon replaced the expensive bronze cannons that the Germans and Italians had been making.

6

There were very few clocks in the Middle Ages and these were usually huge ones on public buildings. The invention of springs made it possible to make watches that could be carried around and also small clocks that people could keep at home. Pendulum clocks were also invented at this time.

7

During the 16th century, the invention and improvement of instruments like these helped sailors to steer their ships more accurately. To make the most of these instruments a captain had to know the stars and be good at mathematics. Gradually, new and better maps were produced too.

Medicine

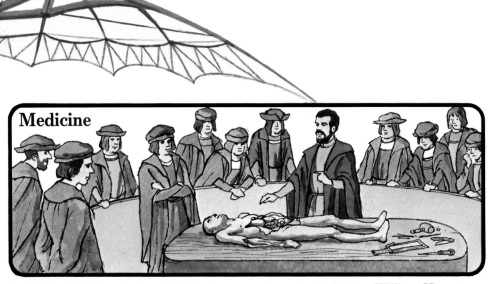

In 1543, a Belgian doctor called Andreas Vesalius published a book about how the human body worked. Here he is lecturing to his students at the university in Padua. William Harvey, another great doctor, discovered and proved that the heart pumps blood round the body.

The invention of microscopes made people realize for the first time that the world was full of minute creatures, too small to see unless they are magnified.

1 Ideas about the universe

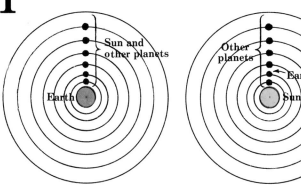

From the time of the Ancient Greeks onwards, people had believed that the Earth was the centre of the universe and that the Sun, Moon and stars moved round it. In 1543, the Polish astronomer, Copernicus, published a book showing that the Sun, not the Earth, was the centre of the universe. Many people refused to believe him.

The invention of the telescope in the early 17th century meant that people could get a better view of the stars and planets. The Italian scientist, Galileo, made a telescope strong enough to show the separate stars of the Milky Way. He supported Copernicus, but the Catholic Church forbade him to teach his theories.

The new interest in science led to the founding of scientific societies. Special places were built, like the Royal Observatory near London, for the study of stars.

This wall has been cut away.

The discoveries of the English scientist, Sir Isaac Newton, changed people's ideas about the universe. Here he is doing an experiment through which he discovered that white light is made up of different colours.

Key dates

AD1444/1510 Italian painter, **Botticelli.**
AD1452/1519 Italian artist/inventor **Leonardo da Vinci.**
AD1454   **Gutenberg** invented his printing press.
AD1466/1536 Dutch scholar **Erasmus.**
AD1469/1527 Italian writer **Machiavelli.**
AD1473/1543 Polish astronomer **Copernicus.**
AD1475/1564 Italian artist **Michelangelo.**
AD1514/1564 Belgian doctor **Vesalius.**
AD1564/1642 Italian astronomer **Galileo.**
AD1578/1657 English doctor **Harvey.**
AD1600   Invention of telescope and
(approx.)   microscope.
AD1642/1727 English scientist **Newton.**

New Ideas About Religion

The people of Western Europe were all Roman Catholics, but by AD1500, many were unhappy with the way the Church was being run. The Popes and many of the priests seemed interested only in wealth and power and set a bad example in the way they lived their lives. This led to a movement, which became known as the "Reformation", to change and reform the Christian Church. People who joined the movement were called "Protestants" because they were protesting about things that they thought were wrong.

In 1517 a German monk called Martin Luther nailed a list of 95 complaints about the Church and the way priests behaved, to the door of Wittenberg church in Germany.

Luther believed that everyone should be able to study God's message for themselves. So he translated the Bible from Latin into German. Versions in other languages quickly followed.

The Catholics fight back

The Pope called a meeting of churchmen at Trent in Italy. They laid down exactly what the beliefs and rules of the Catholic Church were and ordered complete obedience to them.

This is St Ignatius Loyola who founded the Society of Jesus. The members, who were known as Jesuits, tried to win Protestants back to the Catholic Church.

Many Protestants disapproved of decorated churches and destroyed those they took over. But the Catholics introduced an even more elaborate style, shown here, called Baroque.

Murders and executions

Holland was ruled by the Kings of Spain at this time. William of Orange led a revolt of the Dutch Protestants against the Spanish. He was murdered by a Catholic.

So many people in France became Protestants that the Catholics laid a plot. On 24 August 1572, the eve of St Bartholomew's Day, they murdered all the Protestants they could find in Paris.

Mary, Queen of Scots, was a Catholic. She plotted against Elizabeth I, the Protestant Queen of England, and was taken prisoner by the English. She was executed at Fotheringay Castle.

3 Luther was condemned by a Church court, but several German princes supported him. He also won followers across Europe.

4 King Henry VIII of England wanted to divorce his wife and marry Anne Boleyn. The Pope would not let him, so Henry made himself head of the Church in England.

5 Soon there were other religious leaders and the Protestants split into different groups. This is John Calvin, who set up a new Church in Geneva.

6 Priests on both sides were tortured and even hanged. Both Protestants and Catholics believed they were saving their opponents from hell by doing this.

4

In Spain, the most fiercely Catholic country in Europe, there was an organization called the Inquisition, which hunted out anyone who was not a good Catholic. The officers of the Inquistion used torture to make people confess their beliefs. Protestants who refused to become Catholics were burnt to death at special ceremonies called "Auto-da-fe" (Spanish for "acts of faith"), which were watched by huge crowds.

This is a map of Europe in about AD1600. It shows which areas were still Catholic and which had become Protestant.

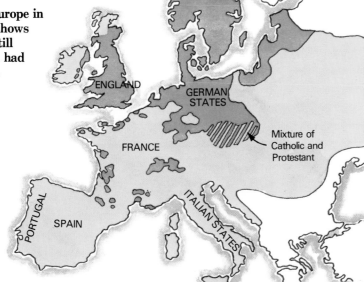

 Protestant

 Catholic

ENGLAND
GERMAN STATES
FRANCE
Mixture of Catholic and Protestant
PORTUGAL
SPAIN
ITALIAN STATES

Key dates

AD1483/1546	Life of **Martin Luther**.
AD1517	Luther nailed 95 theses to Wittenburg church door.
AD1534	**Henry VIII** became head of the Church of England.
	Ignatius Loyola founded the Jesuits (Society of Jesus).
AD1536	**John Calvin** began work in Geneva.
AD1545/1563	The Council of Trent.
AD1555	Fighting between Catholics and Protestants in Germany ended by treaty called Peace of Augsburg.
AD1572	The Massacre of St. Bartholomew's Eve.
AD1584	**William of Orange** was assassinated.
AD1587	**Mary, Queen of Scots**, was executed.

War and Weapons

Guns were invented at the beginning of the 14th century. It was many years before they came into general use, but over the next few centuries they completely changed the way wars were fought. The knights and castles of the Middle Ages gradually disappeared. Their armour was no protection against bullets, so they could not get close enough to the enemy to use their swords and lances. Castle walls could not stand up to an attack of cannon balls.

From about 1300 onwards, archers started using longbows which were very effective against knights. They had a long range and were quite accurate.

Castles and walled towns had been very difficult to capture, but when cannons began to be used in the 15th century, even the thickest walls could be quickly battered down.

Armour and weapons were expensive. When peasants rebelled, as they often did in the 15th and 16th centuries, they had little chance against well-armed knights and nobles. This is a German knight charging a peasant.

When hand-guns were first invented they took a long time to load and were not very accurate. Pikemen were positioned next to the gunmen to protect them against charging cavalry while they reloaded.

Then guns called muskets were invented. They fired more accurately but at first they were too heavy to hold. The musketeers had to use forked sticks to support their guns.

Pistols were less accurate than muskets and fired a shorter distance. They were usually used by cavalry who rode at the enemy, fired at them and rode away to reload.

Towards the end of the 17th century soldiers started to use bayonets (blades which attach to the end of a gun). Gunmen could now defend themselves at close-quarters.

8

Instead of relying on their nobles to raise armies, or hiring mercenary soldiers, kings began to set up permanent armies of their own. These armies were much more highly-trained than before and could obey orders at speed. Commanders had to study hard to learn how to plan their battles and campaigns.

9

War at sea changed too. The Dutch and English developed lighter ships which could turn much more quickly. This helped the English fleet to defeat the Spanish Armada.

10

On ships, cannons were placed along each side. Enemies tried to fire "broadside" at each other so they would have more chance of hitting their target.

11

Disease, bad food and harsh punishments made life at sea very hard. Governments often used "press-gangs" to kidnap men for the navy and take them to sea by force.

Key dates

AD1455/1485 **Wars of the Roses**: civil war in England.

AD1494/1559 **Italian Wars**: Italian states fighting each other. France and the Holy Empire joined in.

AD1524/1525 **Peasants' War** in Germany: the German peasants rebelled.

AD1562/1598 **Wars of Religion in France**: fighting between French Catholics and Protestants.

AD1568/1609 **Dutch Revolt**: the Dutch rebelled against their Spanish rulers.

AD1588 The **Spanish Armada** was defeated by the English fleet.

AD1618/1648 **Thirty Years War**: fought mainly in Germany. Involved most of the countries of Europe.

AD1642/1649 **Civil War** in England.

AD1648/1653 **Wars of the "Fronde"**: two rebellions against the French government.

AD1652/1654, **Wars between the Dutch and**
1665/1667 & **the English.** Fought at sea.
1672/1674 Caused by rivalry over trade.

AD1701/1714 **War of the Spanish Succession**: France and Spain against England, Austria and Holland.

AD1733/1735 **War of the Polish Succession**: Austria and Russia against France and Spain about who should rule Poland.

AD1740/1748 **War of the Austrian Succession**: Austria, Britain and Russia against France and Prussia.

The Incas

The Incas lived in the mountains of Peru in South America. Their capital was a city called Cuzco. From about 1440 onwards they began to conquer neighbouring lands and build up a huge empire. The empire lasted about a hundred years before Spanish soldiers arrived in search of gold and conquered them.

White llamas to be sacrificed.

Temple

Atahualpa

Body of Huayna Capac

Musicians with drums, rattles and flutes.

The emperor of the Incas was called the Inca. His people thought he was descended from the Sun and when he died his body was preserved and treated with great honour.

This is the funeral procession of an emperor called Huayna Capac. His son, Atahualpa, became the new emperor by fighting his half-brother, Huascar.

Unfortunately this war, was just before the Spaniards arrived and it greatly weakened the Incas in their fight against the European invaders.

1 Inca priests were very important people. They held services, heard confessions and foretold the future by looking into the fire. The Sun was their chief god.

2 Women were taught how to weave and spin wool. Some women, who were specially chosen for their beauty, became priestesses called the Virgins of the Sun.

3 The Incas were very skilled at making things out of gold. This gold glove was found in a tomb. Beside it is a model of a god, set with precious stones.

A farming village

Land has been terraced so that crops can be grown on the steep mountainside.

Peasants dig fields with pointed sticks.

Buildings made with heavy blocks of stone have been put together without the help of machinery or iron tools.

Villagers eat mainly maize and vegetables.

Women weaving

Guinea pigs are kept for food.

Men drinking "chicha" beer

Quito

Cuzco

PACIFIC OCEAN

INCA EMPIRE

Keeping records

The Incas had no system of writing but their officials used "quipus" to help them record things. Coloured strings stood for objects. Knots tied in the strings stood for numbers.

All the land belonged to the Inca. One third of the crops was kept by peasants, who lived in mountain villages, like this one, and worked on the land. Another third went to the priests and the last third went to the Inca. With his share he paid his officials, soldiers and craftsmen.

Roads and messengers

A well-maintained network of roads linked all parts of the huge Inca empire. There were hanging bridges, made of twisted straw and vines, across the mountain chasms. These roads and bridges were built and repaired by peasants sent from their villages to serve the emperor. There were no wheeled vehicles so goods were carried by llamas and relays of fast runners carried messages and quipus across the empire. There were rest houses, a day's journey apart, for people on official business to stay in.

The Discovery of America

Until the end of the 15th century, Europeans did not know that the huge continent of America existed. Explorers and traders had made long and difficult journeys eastwards to China and India, bringing back spices, silks and jewels. These were in such demand in Europe that people thought there might be a quicker way to the Far East by sea. The Portuguese sailed to the east round Africa, but others thought it might be quicker to go westwards. When they did, they found America in the way.

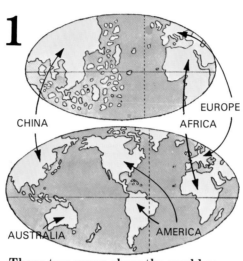

1

These two maps show the world as people in Europe thought it looked in about 1490 (top) and as it really looked (bottom).

An Italian, called Christopher Columbus, persuaded King Ferdinand and Queen Isabella of Spain to pay for an expedition to find China by sailing west instead of east. He set off in 1492 with three ships.

1 The Spanish conquerors

Spanish adventurers ("conquistadors") started to explore the mainland, hoping to find treasure. They discovered the Aztecs in Mexico and the Incas in Peru.

Spanish soldiers, led by Hernando Cortes, attacked the Aztecs in their capital city, Tenochtitlan. Although there were fewer of them, the Spaniards had much better weapons than the Indians, who had never seen horses before. The Spaniards soon conquered the whole of Mexico and called it New Spain.

With the help of his Indian interpreter, Dona Marina, Cortes won the support of several Indian tribes, who helped him to defeat the Aztecs.

In Peru, the Spanish, led by Pizarro, captured the Inca emperor. To buy his freedom he filled a room with gold. But he was killed and Peru conquered.

The Spanish tried to make all the Indians become Christians. Indians who went on worshipping their own gods were burnt to death.

The Spaniards treated the Indians very cruelly. Many were put to work in silver mines. Thousands died of illnesses brought over from Europe.

After five weeks, Columbus reached what he thought were islands off China but were, in fact, the West Indies. Later, he made three more voyages and reached the mainland of America.

To stop Spain and Portugal fighting about who owned the newly discovered lands, the Pope drew a line on the map. All new lands east of the line went to Portugal, those to the west went to Spain.

There were many expeditions to explore the new lands. The first to sail round South America was led by Magellan. He was killed on the way, but his ship returned and was the first to sail right round the world.

Slave trade

The Spanish and Portuguese brought ships full of Africans over to work as slaves. They tried to stop other countries joining in this trade, but some captains, like the Englishman John Hawkins, ignored their ban.

Pirates

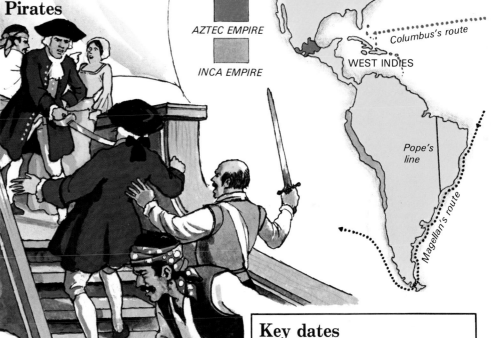

AZTEC EMPIRE

INCA EMPIRE

Columbus's route

WEST INDIES

Pope's line

Magellan's route

Spanish treasure ships were often attacked by pirates on their way back to Spain. The French and English governments even encouraged their sea-captains to be pirates, rewarding them for bringing back treasure.

Key dates

AD1492	First voyage of **Christopher Columbus**.
AD1494	The Pope divided the new lands between Spain and Portugal.
AD1498	**Vasco da Gama** sailed round Africa and reached India.
AD1500	**Pedro Cabral** claimed Brazil for the Portuguese government.
AD1519/1522	**Magellan's** voyage round the world.
AD1519	**Hernando Cortes** landed in Mexico.
AD1521	Fall of Aztec capital, Tenochtitlan.
AD1533	Murder of the Inca, **Atahualpa**.
AD1562/1568	**John Hawkins** shipping African slaves to Spanish America.

Muslim Empires

From about 1300, a Muslim* people called the Ottoman Turks began to build up an empire. In 1453 they captured Constantinople, the centre of the Orthodox Christian Church, and renamed the city Istanbul. Its great cathedral, St Sophia, shown here, became a mosque.

The Ottomans wanted to conquer Europe. Led by Sultan, Suleiman the Magnificent, they defeated the Hungarian army at the Battle of Mohács, and took control of Hungary. They continued to threaten Europe until 1683, when they besieged Vienna and were heavily defeated.

The Sultan's palace

Slaves

This is a slave. The Ottomans chose boys from the Christian areas of their empire, took them away from their families and brought them up as Muslims.

Most of the boys were trained to be soldiers called Janissaries. They were the best troops in the Ottomans' army.

The cleverest of these boys were given a good education, and later they were made government officials.

The Ottoman Sultans spent much of their time in the Topkapi Saray, their splendid palace in Istanbul. Here the Sultan is receiving an envoy from Europe. European princes were eager to buy Turkish goods and make alliances with the Turks.

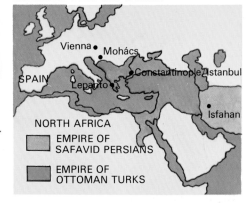

NORTH AFRICA

EMPIRE OF SAFAVID PERSIANS

EMPIRE OF OTTOMAN TURKS

*Muslims belong to a religion called Islam.

Muslims in Persia

1

The Persians, like the Ottomans, were Muslims, but they belonged to a different group of Muslims, called the Shi'ites. This mosque is in Isfahan, their capital city.

2

The Persians and Ottomans often fought each other over religion and land. Their wars lasted on and off for over 200 years.

3

The royal family of Persia was called the Safavids. During the reign of their greatest shah (king), Abbas I, the luxuries of Persia became famous throughout the world.

1 Spain and the Muslims

Muslims had overrun Spain in the 8th century. They were finally driven out when King Ferdinand and Queen Isabella conquered Granada, the last Muslim kingdom in Spain.

2

Some Muslims stayed on in Spain and became Christians. But the Spaniards never trusted them and years later their descendants were banished.

3

The Spanish wanted to keep the Ottomans out of the Mediterranean Sea. In 1571, they defeated them in the great Battle of Lepanto.

4

Fierce pirates from North Africa raided the coasts of Spain and other European countries and carried off people to sell as slaves in Muslim lands.

The Habsburgs

SPANISH HABSBURG LANDS

AUSTRIAN HABSBURG LANDS

The Habsburgs were the most powerful ruling family in Europe in the 16th century. They were the rulers of Austria and most of Central Europe and in 1516 the Habsburg Archduke, Charles V, inherited Spain and the newly won Spanish territories in America too. When Charles died, his empire was divided between his son, Philip II of Spain, and his brother Ferdinand, Archduke of Austria, and from then on Spain and Austria were ruled by separate branches of the Habsburg family.

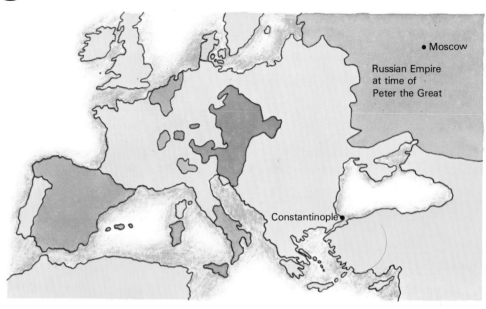

Moscow

Russian Empire at time of Peter the Great

Constantinople

Fabulous riches were sent to Spain from South America, but wars against the French, the Protestants and the Turks cost so much that the kings of Spain were always in debt.

You can see some of the magnificent clothes worn at the Spanish court in the paintings of Velasquez, King Philip IV's court artist. This is Philip's daughter, Margarita Teresa.

The Spanish kings were strong supporters of the Catholic Church. They encouraged the Inquisition to find and punish heretics and declared war on Protestant countries.

At this time there were many famous writers and artists in Spain. This is Don Quixote with his servant Sancho Panza, from the book *Don Quixote* written by Miguel de Cervantes.

Holy Roman Emperors

This is the Holy Roman Emperor, who was elected by a group of seven German princes. They always elected the Habsburg Archduke of Austria because the Habsburgs were so powerful. This meant that the

Archduke ruled over the hundreds of different German states. This was a difficult task as many of the German princes had become Protestant and resented having a Catholic ruler.

The Tsars

Before 1450, Russia was divided into several different states, each with its own ruler. During the 15th century, the Grand Prince of Moscow gradually gained control of all the states. The Russians belonged to the Orthodox Christian Church, which had its centre at Constantinople. But when the Turks, who were Muslims, conquered Constantinople in 1453, Moscow saw itself as the centre of the Orthodox Church.

1 Grand Prince Ivan III of Moscow was the first to use the title "Tsar" and have this double-headed eagle as his emblem.

2 Ivan III ordered that Moscow's fortress, the Kremlin, should be rebuilt. He brought in Italian architects who built the cathedral, shown here, inside its walls.

3 Ivan IV (1533/1584), often known as Ivan the Terrible because of his cruelty, won great victories over the Tartars and also gained control of all the Russian nobles.

He encouraged trade with Europe and is here receiving envoys from Elizabeth I of England.

4 When Ivan the Terrible died, the nobles fought for power until a national assembly chose Michael Romanov, shown here, to be the Tsar.

Peter the Great

Tsar Peter the Great (1689-1725) wanted Russia to become a powerful modern state. He forced his nobles to become more European by making them cut their beards off.

Peter went to Holland and England to learn about ship-building. He brought European craftsmen back with him to build him a strong, new navy.

In 1709, Peter led the Russians to a great victory over Sweden, their main rival, at the Battle of Poltava.

Peter wanted Russia to have the grandest capital city in Europe, so he built St Petersburg (now Leningrad) on the edge of the Baltic Sea.

The Elizabethans

From 1485 to 1603, England was ruled by a family called the Tudors. The best-known of the Tudor rulers are Henry VIII, who separated the English Church from the Roman Catholic, and his daughter, Elizabeth I. When Elizabeth was only three, her mother, Anne Boleyn, was executed. During the reigns of her half-brother Edward VI and half-sister Mary, Elizabeth's life was often in danger, but she survived to become one of England's most brilliant rulers.

This is a painting of Elizabeth. She reigned for 45 years, keeping a magnificent court where she inspired writers, artists and explorers. She never married.

This is a Protestant preacher. Elizabeth declared that the Church of England was Protestant, but she did not persecute people who had other beliefs unless they plotted against her.

Explorers

This is Sir Walter Raleigh. He introduced tobacco and potatoes to England from America. He also tried to start a colony in America, but it was unsuccessful.

Some explorers tried to find a way to the Far East by sailing north-west or north-east. They all failed because their ships could not break through the ice.

Once the explorers had discovered new lands and sea-routes, merchants banded together to form companies to trade overseas, licensed by the government.

The Globe theatre

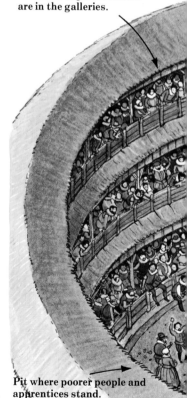

The more expensive seats are in the galleries.

Pit where poorer people and apprentices stand.

The theatre is built of wood with a thatched roof so there is always a danger of fire. (It did, in fact, burn down in 1613.)

Francis Drake

Francis Drake was a great sailor who led daring attacks on Spanish ships and colonies in South America and captured a lot of treasure from them. The Spaniards hated him, but after he had sailed round the world the queen had him knighted on his ship, the Golden Hind. Later, when the Spaniards sent an Armada (fleet) to invade England, Drake played a leading part in their defeat.

3 By avoiding expensive wars, Elizabeth helped England become very wealthy. The nobles and middle classes spent their money on splendid houses, furniture and clothes.

4 Beggars and thieves were a terrible problem. A new law was made which said that all districts must provide work for the poor and shelter those who could not work.

Key dates

AD1505/1585 **Thomas Tallis'** life.
AD1540/1623 **William Byrd's** life.
AD1547/1619 **Nicholas Hilliard's** life.
AD1555   Muscovy company given licence to trade with Russia.
AD1563   Elizabethan Church settlement.
AD1564/1616 **William Shakespeare's** life.
AD1577/1580 **Francis Drake** sailed round the world.
AD1584   **Walter Raleigh** set up colony in Virginia.
AD1588   Defeat of Spanish Armada.
AD1597   Globe theatre opened.
AD1600   East India Company given first licence.
AD1601   Poor Law.

Portraits

We know what many famous Elizabethans looked like from the miniature portraits by an artist called Nicholas Hilliard. This is a picture he painted of himself.

Musicians

Several great musicians lived at this time. Two of the most famous were Thomas Tallis and William Byrd. They composed music to be played at home as well as a great deal of church music.

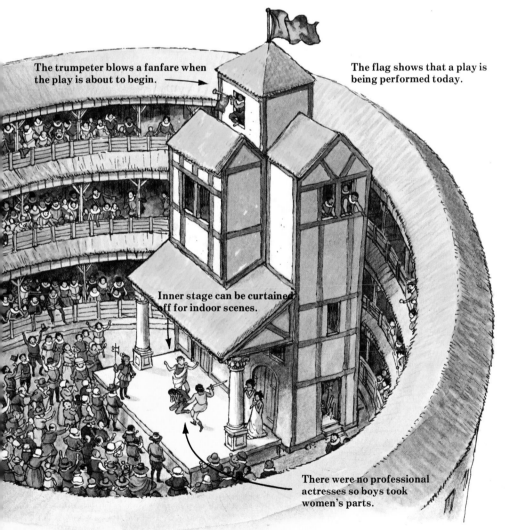

The trumpeter blows a fanfare when the play is about to begin.

The flag shows that a play is being performed today.

Inner stage can be curtained off for indoor scenes.

There were no professional actresses so boys took women's parts.

The Globe in London was the most famous of the theatres built at this time. The first one was opened in 1576. Before this, plays were performed in inn courtyards and town squares.

Shakespeare was an actor and writer with one of the London companies. He wrote at least 36 plays and many of them were first performed at the Globe theatre.

European Settlers

An Indian village

Land cleared by burning.

Boys fishing

Chief

Long houses made of bark.

Party of hunters bringing a deer home.

Palisade made of tree trunks.

Ritual dance

When the first Europeans arrived in North America, there were hundreds of different tribes of native people there. Each had their own customs, language and way of life. Those on the east coast, where the settlers first landed, were farmers, hunters and food gatherers. They lived in small villages and grew corn and some vegetables. This picture is based on drawings made by some of the early European settlers. The arrival of Europeans in the early 17th century was a disaster for these Indians. Many of them died of diseases brought from Europe and many others were killed or driven from their lands.

13 colonies

Mississippi River

The Appalachian Mountains

New England

Boston

Jamestown

Louisiana

In 1607 a group of English settlers set up a colony at Jamestown in Virginia. Here, their leader, Captain John Smith, is being rescued from death by Pocahontas, the daughter of the local Indian chief.

Another group of English people, who became known as the Pilgrim Fathers, sailed to America in 1620 in the ship, "Mayflower". They were Puritans, who wanted freedom to worship God in their own way.

3 The Puritans called the area where they settled New England. During their first winter they had a terrible struggle getting enough food.

4 Local Indians helped the English to survive. After their first harvest they held a feast to thank God. "Thanksgiving Day" is still celebrated in America.

5

Many other Europeans sailed with their families and belongings to live in America. Here is a ship full of settlers unloading. Some of them went because they wanted religious freedom, some were escaping from troubles at home and others came in the hope of finding adventure, or a better life and land of their own. The settlers on the east coast soon formed 13 colonies, each with their own laws and system of government. Gradually they were all brought under the control of the British government.

6 Most colonists settled down as farmers, at first. It was hard work clearing the land, growing crops and defending themselves against hostile Indians.

7 In the south the colonists started growing tobacco. There was a craze for it in Europe so they grew rich by making African slaves work for them.

8 Trade with Europe became profitable and some of the money was used to build towns. This is part of 18th century Boston.

9 A few people, mainly Frenchmen, chose to live as trappers and hunters. They explored along the Mississippi River, claiming land for France.

Plantations and Trading Forts

1 West Indies

Plantation owner

Sugar cane

Overseer

From the 1620s onwards, most of the islands known as the West Indies were taken over by the French and English. They set up sugar plantations and imported African slaves to work on them.

2

Fierce pirates infested the Caribbean Sea at this time. One English pirate called Henry Morgan was eventually knighted by King Charles II.

Key dates

AD1497	**John Cabot** discovered Newfoundland.
AD1523	French begin to explore Canada.
AD1607	English colony set up in Virginia.
AD1608	French founded the settlement of Quebec.
AD1612	First English colony in West Indies set up on Bermuda.
AD1620	The Pilgrim Fathers sailed to America in the Mayflower.
AD1655	English captured Jamaica from Spaniards.
AD1682	The French set up settlements in Louisiana.
AD1759	**General James Wolfe** captured Quebec from the French.
AD1763	Treaty of Paris. England took over Canada from French.

Canadian trading fort

BRITISH

SPANISH

FRENCH

Hudson's Bay Company

Quebec

CANADA

WEST INDIES

JAMAICA

CARIBBEAN SEA

Many French and English people settled in Canada. Some of them were farmers but many of them made a living by trapping animals for fur and catching and salting fish, especially cod. The trappers sold their catch and bought supplies at forts set up by trading companies. The fish and furs were then sent to Europe where they were in great demand.

The capture of Quebec

The lands belonging to England's Hudson Bay Company in Canada and the 13 colonies in America were separated by the French colonies in Canada. From the 1680s onwards, rivalry between the French and British grew and fighting broke out. Here British troops, led by general Wolfe, are reaching the top of the very steep cliffs above the St Lawrence River before making a surprise attack on the French city of Quebec. After the capture of Quebec, the English went on to gain control of the whole of Canada.

The Kingdom of Benin

1 Today Benin is a small town in Nigeria, but between AD1450 and AD1850 it was the capital city of a great kingdom. European explorers brought back reports that Benin's warriors were highly disciplined and very brave, and were constantly fighting to win more land and slaves.

2 The people of Benin had no system of writing, but they made bronze plaques to record important events. This plaque shows their king, who was called the Oba, sacrificing a cow. The Obas spent most of their time in religious ceremonies and let their counsellors govern.

3 The Portuguese were the first Europeans to explore the coast of Africa. Soon others came, eager to buy ivory, gold and especially slaves sold by the local chiefs.

4 The most promising boys were trained as hunters. If they were very good they could become elephant hunters, armed with blow-guns and poisonous darts.

5 Benin lost its power in the 19th century, but the people still survive. This present-day chief is dressed for a festival in honour of the Oba's father.

Music

This carving shows a drummer playing at a ceremony at the Oba's court. The musicians of Benin also played bells and elephant-tusk trumpets.

Carvings

The people of Benin made beautiful portrait heads, like this one of a queen mother. It was the queen mother's duty to bring up the Oba's heir.

There were many skilled craftsmen in Benin. Besides bronze plaques and portrait heads, they made lovely things from ivory, like the bracelets, shown above.

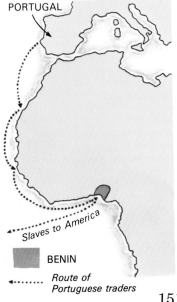

PORTUGAL

Slaves to America

BENIN

Route of
Portuguese traders

151

The Mogul Empire

Muslim warriors had been invading and setting up kingdoms in India since before the 10th century. The most famous Muslim invaders were the Moguls, who were descended from the Mongols. In 1526, they founded the great Mogul Empire in north-west India which lasted until 1858. During their rule, great progress was made in the arts and sciences. Most Indians continued to work on the land, however, as their ancestors had done for centuries before them.

This is the first Mogul emperor, Babur (1526-1530). He was a descendent of the Mongol chiefs, Tamerlane and Genghis Khan.

This is the court of Babur's grandson, Akbar (1556-1605), greatest of the Mogul emperors. He was a good soldier and a wise ruler. He encouraged artists and brought scholars of all religions together to try to find one religion.

The Moguls were strongly influenced by Persian art and learning. This is Akbar's son, whose wife was Persian. Her name, Nurjahan, meant "Light of the World".

Many wonderful buildings were put up by the Moguls. The most famous is the Taj Mahal. It was built by Emperor Shah Jahan, as a tomb for his wife Mumtaz Mahal.

The Mogul emperors and nobles enjoyed hunting. Sometimes they used cheetahs for hunting gazelle. They also hunted tigers while riding on the backs of elephants.

European merchants came to India to buy silks, cotton, ivory, dyes and spices. Gradually they set up trading posts throughout India.

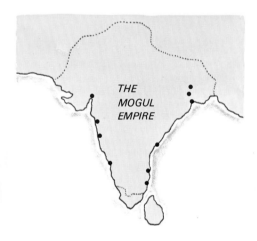

As the power of the Mogul rulers grew weaker, the British and French used the rivalry of lesser princes to increase their own power. Here, one of the princes is preparing for battle.

THE MOGUL EMPIRE

• BRITISH AND FRENCH TRADING POSTS

Ming and Ch'ing Emperors

The emperors of China lived in Peking, in a fantastic palace called the "Forbidden City". Here they were surrounded by richly decorated buildings and lovely gardens. The

Ming dynasty (family line) of emperors (AD1368/1644) cut themselves off from the government and let their officials rule for them. In AD1644 the last Ming emperor

committed suicide and the Ch'ing dynasty won power. They ruled until AD1911. Many of the Ch'ing emperors were clever rulers and brought peace and prosperity to China.

1

This figure, carved in ivory, represents a public official. To obtain this job he had to take a series of very difficult exams.

2

Chinese doctors knew how to prepare medicines by boiling up herbs. They also treated patients by sticking needles in them (acupuncture).

3

Here is a scene from *The Water Margin.* This was one of China's few novels. It tells a story about bandits who protected the poor against wicked officials.

4

European missionaries, like these Jesuit priests were, at first, welcomed by the emperors, but later they were driven out.

5

Porcelain   Silk

Lacquer

Jade   Tea

Many people in Europe wanted to buy beautifully-made Chinese goods, like these. But Europeans had to pay in gold and silver because China did not want European goods.

Farming

In the countryside life continued with few changes. New crops, such as maize, were introduced from America by Spanish and Portuguese traders. During the period of peace under the

Ch'ing emperors the population began to increase. At first this did not matter, but later, it became difficult to grow enough grain to feed everyone.

153

Life in Japan

The emperors of Japan were greatly honoured, but had no real power. The country was ruled by an official called the Shogun. The first Europeans reached Japan in the 1540s and for nearly a century they traded with the Japanese. But then the Shogun expelled all foreign merchants, except the Chinese and the Dutch, and the Japanese people remained totally cut off from the rest of the world until 1854.

In 1467, civil war broke out. For over 100 years, the local barons, called daimyos, fought each other. They built huge castles like this one, half-fortress, half-palace, where they lived with their warriors, the samurai. The samurai believed that the only honourable way of life was to fight for and give loyal service to their daimyo. Eventually, a powerful daimyo called Tokugawa Ieyasu, succeeded in uniting Japan. He became Shogun and ruled from his capital in Edo (now Tokyo). The Tokugawa family held power until 1868.

1 The ancient Japanese Shinto faith became popular again in the 18th century. Here a new baby is being brought to a Shinto shrine.

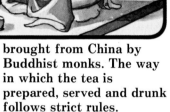

2 Tea drinking developed into an elaborate ceremony, which still plays an important part in Japanese life. Both the ceremony and the tea were originally brought from China by Buddhist monks. The way in which the tea is prepared, served and drunk follows strict rules.

3 Christianity was brought to Japan by Jesuits. They converted many people but later the Shoguns banned Christianity and had many Christians executed.

4 Arranging flowers was a special art, called Ikebana, which at first only men were allowed to do. The type of flowers and the way they are arranged have special meanings.

5 Pictures made by printing from carved blocks of wood became popular at this time. Most of them illustrate the lives of ordinary people.

6 This is a street bookseller in the early 18th century. Poetry and novels were still popular but there were no longer many women writers as there had been earlier.

7 Puppet theatres and a type of musical play called "Kabuki" became very popular. These were livelier and more realistic than older Japanese dramas.

A Dutch island

From 1630 onwards, Dutch merchants had to live on this small island in Nagasaki Bay. They were not expelled completely like other foreigners because the Shoguns felt they would not try to conquer or convert the Japanese. A bridge linked the island to the land, but the Dutch were not allowed to cross it.

Key dates

AD1467/1568	Period of civil war in Japan.
AD1543	First Portuguese traders reached Japan. Other Europeans follow.
AD1549/1551	**St Francis Xavier** working in Japan.
AD1592 & 1597	Japanese invaded Korea.
AD1600/1868	Tokugawa family rule.
AD1603	**Tokugawa Ieyasu** became Shogun.
AD1606/1630	Christians persecuted.
AD1623/1639	All Europeans, except a few Dutch, left Japan.

Merchants and Trade

Once explorers had discovered new lands and sea-routes in the 16th century, there was a huge increase in trade between Europe and the rest of the world. By the 17th century the main trading countries were Holland, England and France. In these countries the merchants and middle classes who organized this trade became very wealthy and began to copy the life-style of the nobles. Even some of the ordinary working people benefited from this increase in wealth.

Groups of merchants, like these, set up trading companies in which people could buy shares. The shareholders' money was used to pay the cost of trading ventures and any profit was divided amongst the shareholders.

Many merchants bought goods from people who worked in their own homes and sold them abroad. Here a merchant's agent is buying cloth from a family workshop.

Companies hired ships to export their goods. Countries competing for overseas trade had to have good ships, sailors and ports. Dutch ships were among the best in Europe.

Rich merchants began to band together to set up banks to lend money. For this service they charged a fee called "interest". People could also bring their money to the bank

for safe-keeping. The first bankers were Italian merchants. In the 17th century London and Amsterdam became the most important banking cities.

In some of the big cities of Europe, coffee houses became the places where people met to buy and sell shares and discuss business.

It soon became more convenient to have a proper building for use as a market where people could buy and sell shares. This is the Amsterdam Stock Exchange, built in 1613. Soon there were stock exchanges like this in all the important trading centres of Europe.

Special insurance companies were set up. Merchants paid them a fee and if their trading expeditions met with disaster the insurance company stood the cost.

1 The new middle classes

As the merchant classes grew richer, they built themselves big town houses. The fashionable areas of big cities had pavements and wide streets.

2

The new middle classes wanted to live like the nobles. Many of them became rich enough to buy country estates and obtained titles. Some of the nobility looked down on them but others were happy to marry into these wealthy families.

3

Governments needed to understand business and finance so sometimes men from the merchant classes were chosen as royal ministers and advisers.

4

We know what many of the Dutch merchants of this time looked like because many of them paid artists to paint their portraits.

5

Many of the paintings of this time, especially Dutch ones, show us how merchant families lived and what their homes looked like.

6

In every country there were still many desperately poor people. Some nobles and merchants tried to help the poor. They founded hospitals, homes for old people and orphanages. Here a group of merchants' wives are inspecting an orphanage run by nuns.

Dutch merchants find Australia

On their trips to the east, Dutch sailors discovered Australia, which they called New Holland. Some people were wrecked there and tried to set up settlements but all their early attempts failed.

The Dutch controlled most of the important spice trade between Europe and the East Indies. This made Holland the greatest trading nation in Europe for much of the 17th century. This map shows the Dutch empire in the East Indies and the things they went there to buy.

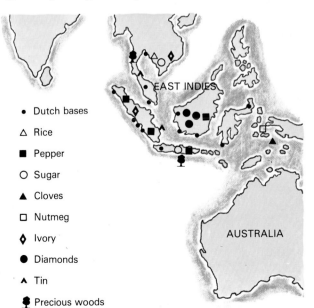

- • Dutch bases
- △ Rice
- ■ Pepper
- ○ Sugar
- ▲ Cloves
- □ Nutmeg
- ◊ Ivory
- ● Diamonds
- ▲ Tin
- ♣ Precious woods

Kings and Parliaments

1

In the 17th and 18th centuries much of Europe was ruled by kings, queens and emperors who were extremely powerful. These rulers are known as "absolute monarchs". The court of

Louis XIV of France was the most brilliant in Europe. This is the Hall of Mirrors in his palace at Versailles. Louis encouraged the French nobles to come and live at his court, and

spend their time in a round of entertainments, so that he could keep an eye on them. Other monarchs built themselves great palaces too and tried to imitate Louis' way of life.

1 **The English parliament**

Parliament supporter ("roundhead")

King's supporter ("cavalier")

King Charles I of England tried to ignore parliament and rule like an absolute monarch. Many people were so unhappy with the way he ruled that in 1642 civil war broke out.

2

The king was defeated and executed. Oliver Cromwell, the leader of the parliamentarian army became ruler. He could not get parliament to agree with him so he too tried to rule without parliament.

3

Oliver Cromwell died in 1658. His son was incompetent and no one would support his government. Eventually Charles I's son was invited back and crowned King Charles II.

2 Parliaments hardly ever met. The king took all the important decisions. His ministers could only advise him and carry out his instructions. In order to keep control a successful ruler, like Louis XIV, had to spend hours every day with his ministers in meetings like this one.

3 Sometimes the king's favourites became very powerful. Louis XV let Madame du Pompadour, shown above, make important decisions.

4 The king made the laws and could put his enemies in prison if he wanted. Law-courts did what the king wanted.

5 Absolute monarchs usually kept large, permanent armies. Frederick the Great of Prussia, which is now part of Germany, was a brilliant military commander. Here he is inspecting his troops.

6 Monarchs often brought great painters, musicians and writers to their courts. As a child, Mozart played the piano at the court of Maria Teresa.

7 To add to the strength of their countries rulers set up industries. Some of these produced luxury goods such as tapestries, silk and glass. This is a glassworks.

4 Parliament's power increased, however, and the king's minister had to have the support of its members. This is Robert Walpole one of the most successful ministers of the 18th century.

5 Members of parliament formed two political parties called the Whigs and the Tories. Only people who owned property worth more than a certain value could vote.

Key dates

AD1642	English Civil War began.
AD1643/1715	**Louis XIV** ruled France.
AD1649	**Charles I** was executed.
AD1658	**Oliver Cromwell** died.
AD1660/1685	Reign of **Charles II.**
AD1682/1725	**Peter the Great** ruled Russia.
AD1715/1774	**Louis XV** ruled France.
AD1730/1741	**Robert Walpole** was Prime Minister.
AD1740/1780	**Maria Teresa** ruled Austria.
AD1740/1786	**Frederick the Great** ruled Prussia (now part of Germany).
AD1756/1791	Life of **Mozart**.
AD1762/1796	**Catherine the Great** ruled Russia.

Sports and Pastimes

In the 16th century, nobles and kings played an early version of tennis on special courts. Bowls were also a favourite game at this time.

A cruel but popular sport was cock-fighting. Cocks were specially trained to fight, often to the death. The crowd placed bets on which bird would win.

Fox-hunting was a sport for the wealthy. Horse-racing, which was introduced later on, interested a wider audience.

All classes of people liked to watch bear or bull baiting. The animal was put in a ring and fierce dogs set onto it to kill it. Often some of the dogs got killed as well.

The English village of Hambledon had the first recognized cricket club. The game was later introduced to many of the countries in the British Empire.

Special gambling houses were set up where people could gamble on cards and dice. Huge sums of money would change hands every evening.

Fencing and shooting were sports, but gentlemen sometimes killed each other in duels with swords or pistols, fought over an insult or gambling quarrel.

Boxing grew in popularity, particularly in the early years of the 19th century. Many young noblemen learned to box, but did not fight in public contests.

In the late 18th century, sea-bathing became fashionable for people who could afford to travel to the coast.

They used "bathing machines" to stop people watching them from the beach.

Pirates, Highwaymen and Smugglers

During the 18th century traders and explorers on long sea trips were likely to be attacked by bands of pirates, who sailed the seas looking for ships to plunder. The West Indies, where many pirates hid among the islands, was an especially dangerous area.

Travel by land was slow, uncomfortable and dangerous. The roads were not made up and coaches sometimes overturned.

There were highwaymen too, who held up the coaches and demanded the passengers' money and valuables.

European countries charged taxes, called customs duties, on goods brought into the country. To avoid paying the taxes, smugglers worked secretly, often at night, bringing brandy, silks and other expensive goods from ships moored off the shore.

Towns and villages along the coast had Coast Guards and Excise Officers whose job it was to look out for smugglers. Once onshore the goods had to be hidden until they could be sold. You can still see old inns with secret cellars where smuggled goods were hidden.

When countries such as Britain and France were at war, trade between them was supposed to stop, but the smugglers went on carrying the goods and made great profits. If they were caught they were severely punished and sometimes even hung.

A Revolution in Farming

In the 18th century farming methods in England changed completely. The experiments of a few enthusiastic landowners led to the invention of new tools, the introduction of new crops and new ways of improving the soil and breeding better animals. Landowners found it easier to introduce improvements if they gave each farmer a block of land, instead of thin strips in different fields as was usual then. These changes, known as the "Agricultural Revolution", later happened in other parts of Europe.

By using only their best animals for breeding, farmers produce much bigger, healthier animals.

New crops, like turnips and clover are stored in barns, so animals can now be kept and fed over the winter instead of being killed.

Most villagers cannot produce enough food for themselves, now that the common land has been divided up. They have sold their land and now work for other farmers for wages.

Clergyman's house

Village inn

Hedges have been planted round the fields.

The village green is all that is left of the old common (land which could be used by all the villagers), which has been shared out as farmland.

The landowner built these cottages for villagers who work for him.

Vegetable plot

On pages 104 and 105, you can see what this village looked like in the Middle Ages.

Village windmill for grinding corn.

House of chief landowner of the village, often called the squire. Some other villagers own their land, but he still owns the most.

This carrier has just delivered some goods to the house.

New plough cuts deeper furrows.

Seed drill sows seeds in straight lines.

Doctor's house

Animal manure is spread on the land to make it more fertile.

Ditch for draining land that used to be too wet for growing crops.

Landowner (squire)

Blacksmith

This farmer owns the land he farms.

This family is leaving to go and work in a town.

Village shop

Hoeing keeps the crop free of weeds so there will be a bigger harvest.

Milkmaid

Woman spinning

Landowner's wife

This man rents a farm from the landowner.

In this field the farmer grows wheat one year, turnips the next, barley the third year and clover the fourth. This order of growing crops keeps the field fertile. Fields are no longer left unplanted every third year.

163

Machines and Factories

In the first half of the 18th century, most people in Britain still lived and worked in the countryside. Woollen and cotton cloth, produced in the north of England, were the chief manufactured goods. Before 1750 cloth was mainly made by hand, in people's homes. But by 1850 it was being made by machines in factories. The new factories employed lots of people and towns quickly grew up round them. These changes in working life have become known as the "Industrial Revolution".

1 Making cloth

Spinning Weaving

Combing wool ready for spinning.

Britain produced a great deal of woollen cloth. In the first half of the 18th century, most of it was made by villagers in their homes and sold to visiting merchants.

2

Then machines like this were invented. They helped spinners and weavers to work much faster. Later they were adapted to be driven by water, and later still by steam.

Steam power

This is one of Watt's steam engines.

The early factories used water power to make their machines go. Various people experimented with the idea of using steam. Eventually a Scotsman called James Watt found out how to make steam engines drive the wheels of other machines and these were soon being used in factories.

Iron

This is an iron works. Iron was needed for making the new machines, but iron-smelting needed charcoal and the wood for making this was in short supply.

Coal was no good as its fumes made the iron brittle. Then, Abraham Darby discovered coal could be turned into coke which was pure enough for making iron.

1 Coal

People had been using coal to heat their homes for a long time, but it had been dug only from shallow mines. Deep mines were too dangerous.

2

Safety lamp

Several inventions made mining safer. The safety lamp cut down the danger of explosions. Steam pumps helped prevent flooding and there was also a machine which sucked out stale air.

3

Underground rails made it easier to haul coal to the surface from great depths, but conditions in the mines were still very bad. Small children were used to pull the heavy trucks.

164

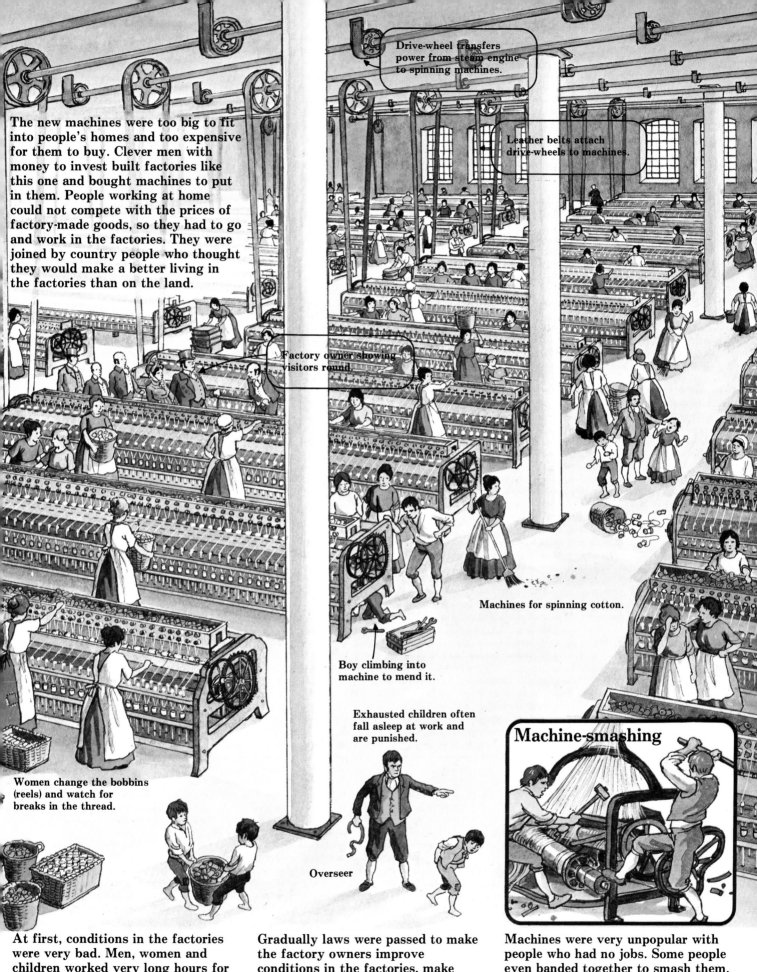

Drive-wheel transfers power from steam engine to spinning machines.

Leather belts attach drive-wheels to machines.

The new machines were too big to fit into people's homes and too expensive for them to buy. Clever men with money to invest built factories like this one and bought machines to put in them. People working at home could not compete with the prices of factory-made goods, so they had to go and work in the factories. They were joined by country people who thought they would make a better living in the factories than on the land.

Factory owner showing visitors round.

Machines for spinning cotton.

Boy climbing into machine to mend it.

Exhausted children often fall asleep at work and are punished.

Women change the bobbins (reels) and watch for breaks in the thread.

Overseer

Machine-smashing

At first, conditions in the factories were very bad. Men, women and children worked very long hours for low wages. Machines had no safety guards and there were bad accidents.

Gradually laws were passed to make the factory owners improve conditions in the factories, make working hours shorter and protect the rights of working people.

Machines were very unpopular with people who had no jobs. Some people even banded together to smash them. One group was called the Luddites after their leader, Ned Ludd.

Life in the New Towns

Where factories were built, new towns quickly grew up to house the factory workers. They were overcrowded and unhealthy places and they caused many problems.

Factory owner's house

Factories

Railway (goods line)

Chimney sweep and apprentice

Policeman

Barrel organ

Hansom cab

Gas lamp

Pickpocket

Fruit-seller

Cheap houses, built back-to-back, were put up for the factory workers, especially in the northern towns. Often there were no toilets or running water. The streets were dirty and the air and rivers polluted by factories.

Diseases spread quickly. Until cheap ways of travelling were developed the workers had to live near the factories, which were often built near coal mines and ironworks.

1 The changes in farming and industry left some people without jobs and desperately poor. To get help they had to go and live in "workhouses". Conditions in the workhouses were very harsh to discourage lazy people from using them. Men and women lived in separate quarters so families were split up. Poor people often preferred to live on the streets.

2 Several reformers tried to help poor people. Dr Barnardo, shown here, set up children's homes and General Booth started a Christian organization called the Salvation Army.

3 Many laws were passed during the 19th century to improve people's lives by cleaning up towns, building better houses and setting up schools where all children could go without paying.

4 Old-age pensions started in 1909. These people are collecting theirs from the post office. In 1911, a law was passed which insured people against sickness and unemployment.

5 Workers began to join together to form trade unions so that they could bargain for better wages and working conditions by threatening to strike. At first the trade unions were illegal but gradually laws were passed which made them legal and gave them the right to picket (stand outside their work places and try to persuade other workers not to go in).

6 Some trade unionists and people who agreed with them formed the Labour Party. In the general election of 1906, 29 of their members were elected to parliament.

Transport and Travel

The Industrial Revolution brought about immense changes in transport and travel. Some important developments happened first in Britain, others happened first in America and other parts of Europe.

1

In England, companies called Turnpike Trusts were set up. They built and repaired roads and charged people tolls for using them. This is one of the tollgates. Engineers, like Telford and Macadam, found ways of building roads with hard surfaces.

2

New bridges were also built, many of them iron. This is the Clifton Suspension Bridge in England, designed by Brunel, a famous engineer.

3

Bicycles were in general use by the 1880s. The early "penny-farthings" were ridden by men, but later models were suitable for women to ride too.

4

As the population increased during the 19th century, cities grew in size. People had to live further from their work and horse-drawn buses were introduced to provide them with transport. Before long, city streets became packed with traffic.

5

The first motor cars were made in Germany in 1885. They remained too expensive for anyone but the very wealthy until the 1920s.

1 Canals

In the 18th century, it was much cheaper to send heavy goods by water than by road. Where there were no suitable rivers, canals were cut to link important ports and cities. Locks, like the ones shown here, took the boats up and down slopes. The barges were pulled by horses walking along the "towpath."

2

In 1869 the Suez Canal, which links the Mediterranean Sea to the Red Sea, was opened. This canal cut several weeks off the journey from Europe to India. Later, in 1915, another long ship canal was opened. This was the Panama Canal in Central America which joined the Atlantic and Pacific Oceans.

Railways

Early type of locomotive designed by famous railway engineer George Stephenson.

The first steam locomotive to run on rails was built in England in 1804 by Richard Trevithick. Twenty years later, the first passenger railway was opened and from then on railways became very popular. They were a quick, cheap and safe way of carrying people and goods. As train services improved, it became possible for ordinary people to go on seaside and country holidays. England's roads and canals were neglected.

London got its first long stretch of underground railway in 1863. Until 1890, when electric trains came in, the underground trains were steam–powered. The tunnels are still filled with the soot they made.

1 Sea travel

2

3

Very fast sailing ships called "clippers" were built during the 19th century and used to carry light cargoes such as tea. A completely new kind of ship was also being developed at this time. These ships were built of iron and had steam-engines. They gradually replaced sailing ships.

Many lighthouses were built and a life-boat service introduced, making sea travel much safer than it had been in the past.

Faster and safer sea travel tempted wealthy people to take holidays abroad. In 1869, Thomas Cook ran his first holiday tour to Egypt.

1 The first flights

2

The French Montgolfier brothers were the first people to take off into the air. This was in 1783 in a hot-air balloon. Other balloonists tried using hydrogen.

At the beginning of the 20th century, two Americans, the Wright brothers, built a glider like this one. Later they built an aeroplane fitted with an engine and in 1903 made the first powered flight.

Key dates

AD1663/1770	Turnpike trusts set up.
AD1783	First ascent of hot air balloon.
AD1804	First steam vehicle to run on rails.
AD1829	First railroads opened in U.S.A.
AD1839	First pedal bicycle made.
AD1863	Opening of first underground railway.
AD1869	Suez Canal opened.
AD1885	**Karl Benz** made a 3-wheeled motor car.
AD1886	**Gottlieb Daimler** made a 4-wheeled motor car.
AD1903	First powered flight.

French Revolution and Napoleon's Wars

1 The King of France, Louis XVI, and his wife, Marie Antoinette, lived in the magnificent palace of Versailles near Paris. Here they were surrounded by rich nobles who hardly paid any taxes. Louis was not a good ruler and they were all unpopular with the people.

2 Many nobles were very arrogant and treated everyone else with scorn. The middle classes were very annoyed by this.

3 The peasants had to pay taxes to the church, the government and their local lord. They also had to work for their lords.

4 By 1789, the government had no more money left, so the king was forced to call a meeting of the States General (parliament), which had not met for 175 years. Later the States General passed many reforms but most people were still not satisfied.

5 On July 14, 1789, a crowd in Paris captured a royal prison called the Bastille. This sparked off riots all over France.

6 The revolution became more violent. The king, queen, nobles and anyone not revolutionary enough were executed by guillotine.

7 European rulers were horrified by events in France and soon the French were at war with most of the rest of Europe. Here a soldier is recruiting people for the French army. Many clever young officers were found, in particular Napoleon Bonaparte.

8 Napoleon was so successful as a military commander that he became First Consul of France and then had himself crowned Emperor.

9 Napoleon gained control of much of Europe. He made his brothers and sisters rulers of the lands he conquered. This map shows the lands ruled by him and members of his family by 1810.

10

Napoleon planned to invade Britain, his most determined enemy. But after the British defeated the French at sea in the Battle of Trafalgar, he gave up the idea.

11

In 1812, Napoleon invaded Russia with an army of 600,000 men. He defeated the Tsar's army and marched to Moscow. But the Russians had set fire to Moscow and removed all the provisions. Here the French army is returning home in the middle of winter. Hundreds of thousands of them died from cold and hunger.

12

After his disastrous invasion of Russia, there was a general reaction against Napoleon in Europe. British troops helped the Spanish to drive the French out of Spain.

The Battle of Waterloo

The Battle of Waterloo was the last great battle in the wars against Napoleon. The French were completely defeated by a British army, led by Wellington, and a Prussian army, led by Blücher.

Louis XVIII was made King of France, and Napoleon was imprisoned on the small British island of St Helena in the South Atlantic Ocean, where he died in 1821.

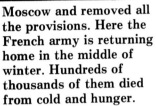

Key dates	
AD1789	First meeting of the States General.
AD1792	France went to war with Austria and Prussia.
AD1793/1794	Period called ''The Reign of Terror''. Hundreds of people guillotined.
AD1804	**Napoleon** became Emperor.
AD1805	Battle of Trafalgar.
AD1808/1814	War between the British and French in Spain and Portugal.
AD1812	**Napoleon's** invasion of Russia.
AD1815	Battle of Waterloo.

New Nations and Ways of Governing

The 18th and 19th centuries were times of great change in the way countries were governed. There were many revolutions and several new, independent nations emerged.

1 Independence for America

In 1775 war broke out. The British Army were far from home and supplies. The colonists were on their own ground and their riflemen were very good shots.

In 1781 the British surrendered at Yorktown and in 1783 they signed a treaty recognizing the United States of America as an independent nation.

Most European settlers in America lived in the 13 colonies* on the east coast. In the early 18th century Britain helped them in their wars against the Indians and the French. The British then taxed them to pay for the wars. The colonists hated the taxes and sometimes attacked British tax officers.

When the new constitution (set of rules by which a country is governed) had been agreed upon, George Washington was chosen as first President of America.

Key Dates

AD1775/1783 War of American Independence.
AD1789/1797 **George Washington** President of the U.S.A.
AD1818/1883 Life of **Karl Marx**.
AD1859/1860 **General Garibaldi** drove French and Austrians out of Italy.
AD1861 Kingdom of Italy founded.
AD1871 German Empire founded. **William I** became Kaiser and **Bismarck** First Chancellor.

Germany

Early in the 19th century Germany was a group of states, the strongest of which was Prussia. In 1861 William I became King of Prussia. With his chief minister, Bismarck, he gradually brought all Germany under his control. In 1871 William was proclaimed Kaiser (emperor) of Germany.

Battleship being launched

Germany became one of the strongest countries in Europe. It quickly built a large navy, developed its industries and won colonies in Africa and the Far East.

Germans became very interested in their country's history. The operas of Wagner based on tales of German gods and heroes, became very popular.

*A colony is a settlement ruled by the country from which the settlers have come.

Italy

In Italy, some states were independent, some were ruled by France and some by Austria. General Garibaldi and his soldiers, known as the "Red Shirts" (above) helped to drive the foreigners out of Italy and make it an independent nation.

ITALY IN 1866

GERMAN EMPIRE IN 1871

1 Ideas about government

In Britain, the people chose which political party should rule by voting at elections. At first few people had the right to vote but gradually it was extended to all men.

2

Some women began to demand the vote. They were called suffragettes.

They held marches and caused as much disturbance as possible to win support.

3

Rulers in many countries were afraid of democracy (people having a say in the running of the country). Soldiers were used against the people who protested.

4

People with revolutionary ideas were sometimes executed or put in prison so they could not lead the people against their ruler.

5

Some people believed any form of government was wrong. They were called anarchists and they killed many political leaders.

6

A German thinker, called Karl Marx, wrote many books with new ideas about government. He wanted people to get rid of their rulers in a revolution and then have new governments run by the working people. Communism is based on his ideas.

173

Slavery and Civil War

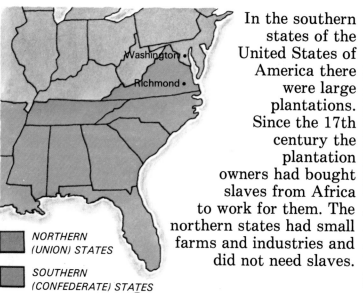

In the southern states of the United States of America there were large plantations. Since the 17th century the plantation owners had bought slaves from Africa to work for them. The northern states had small farms and industries and did not need slaves.

The slave trade became well organized. Europeans either captured Africans or bought them from local rulers, like the King of Dahomey, shown here.

Conditions on the ships carrying the slaves to America were dreadful as the more slaves a trader could get on a ship, the greater his profit.

When they reached America, the slaves who had survived the voyage were sold at auctions. They could be sold again at any time and families were often parted.

Some slaves were lucky enough to work in their master's house but most were used as field hands on the plantation. Most estate owners grew either cotton, tobacco or sugar, all of which need constant attention. Because of the heat African slaves were thought best for this work. Some masters were very cruel but others treated their slaves quite well.

Many slaves tried to escape to the north where they would be free as there was no slavery. A black woman called Harriet Tubman, helped 19 groups of slaves escape.

Protests against slavery began to grow. In 1833 slavery was abolished in the British Empire and the Anti-Slavery Society was founded in America. This is its badge.

In the American Congress (parliament) there were bitter arguments about slavery. The northerners wanted to abolish it but the southerners were determined to keep slaves.

The outbreak of war

In 1861 the southern states elected their own president and broke away from the Union of the United States, declaring themselves a "confederacy" The north thought the states should stay united so war broke out between the Unionists (northerners) and Confederates (southerners). It lasted for four years. There were many fierce battles and nearly 635,000 people lost their lives.

Camp

Mine exploding

Southern (Confederate) flag

Northern (Unionist) flag

Barbed wire

Trench

A new style of fighting developed during the American Civil War. Soldiers made trenches protected by barbed wire. They used mines, hand-grenades and flame throwers.

At first the southerners, led by General Lee, were quite successful. But the north had more soldiers, factories to make weapons and railways to transport them. It used its navy to stop ships bringing supplies to the south. Despite terrible suffering the southerners fought bravely on, but in 1865 they were finally forced to surrender.

1 After the war

President Abraham Lincoln, who had been elected before the war broke out, hoped to make a lasting peace but he was assassinated at Ford's Theater in Washington.

2

The south had been ruined by the war and its main town, Richmond, had been burned. For years afterwards both white and black people were very poor.

3

Some southerners still regarded black people as slaves. They formed a secret society called the Ku Klux Klan. Members covered themselves in sheets and terrorized black people.

Explorers and Empire Builders

In 1750 there were still huge areas of the world where Europeans had never been. During the 19th and late 18th centuries European explorers set out to discover as much as they could about the lands and oceans of the world. Traders and settlers followed and the European countries began to set up colonies abroad which they ruled.

Captain Cook

Captain Cook led three expeditions (1768-79) to the Pacific Ocean. He visited islands such as Tahiti where he was met by war canoes.

He explored the east coast of Australia. Its strange animals fascinated the artists and scientists on the expedition.

He also sailed round the islands of New Zealand. The crew of his ship *Endeavour* landed and met the Maoris who lived there.

1 Exploring Africa

During the 19th century people began to explore and make maps of Africa. They saw wonderful sights such as the Victoria Falls, but many fell ill and died of strange diseases.

2 On a journey in search of the source of the Nile, two British explorers, Speke and Grant, stayed with Mutesa, King of Buganda, who treated them with great hospitality.

3 Some explorers, such as Dr Livingstone, were also Christian missionaries.*Missionaries set up hospitals and schools for the Africans, as well as churches.

4 The Frenchman, René Caillé, was one of the earliest European explorers in the Sahara Desert. He was also one of the first Europeans to see the ancient African city of Timbuktu.

5 There were also several women explorers in the 19th century. This is Alexandrine Tinné, a wealthy Dutch heiress, who travelled through much of North Africa and the Sudan.

*People who went to foreign lands to teach the people about Christianity.

Other expeditions

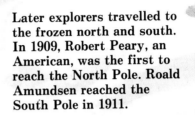

1

Richard Burton was a daring explorer. He disguised himself to visit the Arab holy city, Mecca, where only Muslims were allowed.

2

Many explorers never returned from the jungles of South America where they went to make maps and search for lost cities.

3

Later explorers travelled to the frozen north and south. In 1909, Robert Peary, an American, was the first to reach the North Pole. Roald Amundsen reached the South Pole in 1911.

1 Setting up colonies

Europeans wanted new places to sell their factory-made goods. They also wanted to buy raw materials such as cotton and tea.

2

If quarrels between local rulers threatened trade, the Europeans sent armies. These often stayed after the fighting was over.

3

They also sent officials to organize and govern the territory for them, thus setting up a colony there.

4

More and more Europeans went to the colonies and settled there with their families. They organized vast estates where the local people worked and grew tea, rubber, cotton and foodstuffs or reared sheep and cattle. Later, when minerals were discovered, factories and railways were built and still more people went to live in the colonies.

5

In Europe, politicians were worried by the increase in population and they encouraged people to go and settle in the colonies where there was land and work for them.

Europeans in Africa

1 North Africa

In the early 19th century most of the countries of North Africa were part of the Ottoman Empire*. But the Ottoman Empire was breaking up and European powers began to move in.

The French gained control of Algeria and later Tunisia and Morocco. Here, desert tribesmen are attacking one of the French forts, which is defended by the famous French Foreign Legion.

2

The ruler of Egypt needed money, so he sold his shares in the Suez Canal to Britain. Britain became involved in Egyptian affairs and later took over the government.

3

Egypt also ruled the Sudan. In 1883 a religious leader, the Mahdi, led a revolt. Britain sent an army led by General Gordon, but it was defeated at Khartoum.

Trading in the West

These gold objects were made by the Ashanti, a people who live in west Africa. They grew rich by trading in gold and slaves. They fought the British in several wars and were defeated in 1901.

Zimbabwe

Zimbabwe was the capital city of a rich kingdom in south-east Africa. It was destroyed probably in the early 19th century by rival tribes. The people were clever builders and this is the remains of a temple in the city.

*Empire of Muslim people from Middle East called the Ottoman Turks.

1 South Africa

Dutch settlers had first arrived in South Africa in 1652. They set up Cape Colony on the Cape of Good Hope. Most of them were farmers and they became known as "Boers" (Dutch word for farmers). In 1814 an international treaty gave Cape Colony to the British. The Boers hated being ruled by the British and between 1835 and 1837 many of them set off northwards, with all their possessions in wagons, to find new lands free from British rule. This movement is called the "Great Trek".

Cecil Rhodes

Cecil Rhodes made a fortune from diamond and gold mines, then formed a company to build a railway from the British colony to the mining area north of the Boer states. In 1895 this area became known as Rhodesia.

The Grab for Africa

- FRENCH
- BRITISH
- GERMAN
- PORTUGUESE
- BELGIAN
- SPANISH
- ITALIAN

In 1880 much of Africa was still independent of any European country. Between 1880 and the outbreak of World War I in 1914, the European powers carved up nearly the whole of Africa between them. This map shows Africa in 1914.

2

The Boers came into conflict with the Zulus, the fiercest of the neighbouring African tribes. The British helped the Boers and eventually, in 1879, the Zulus were completely defeated.

3

The British gradually increased their control over the Boer states. In 1886, gold was discovered in one of them and many more British people came out to work in them.

4

In 1899 war broke out between the Boers and the British. The Boers did very well at first. They rode fast horses, were good at stalking the enemy and knew the countryside.

5

The British destroyed the Boers' farms and animals and put all the Boers they could find, including women and children, into special prison camps. In 1902 the Boers surrendered.

Key dates

AD1814	Britain gained control of Cape Colony.
c. AD1830	Collapse of Kingdom of Zimbabwe.
AD1830	French began to take over North Africa.
AD1835/1837	The Great Trek.
AD1875	Britain bought Egypt's shares in the Suez Canal.
AD1878/9	Zulu War.
AD1885	Fall of Khartoum.
AD1896	Britain took over Matabeleland which became Rhodesia.
AD1899/1902	Boer War.
AD1901	Ashanti kingdom became British.
AD1910	Union of South Africa set up.

The British in India

1

This is a court of the British East India Company which started as a trading company. By the 19th century it governed most of India.

2

The British built railways and schools and tried to modernize India. They also tried to stop some of the Indians' religious customs. The Indians resented this interference. In 1857 some *sepoys* (Indian soldiers in the British Army) mutinied and the revolt quickly spread. The British eventually regained control but in future changes were made more carefully.

3

After the Mutiny the East India Company lost its right to rule and the British Government appointed its own officials. Indian princes also lost their power but were very wealthy and still lived in great luxury.

4

Queen Victoria became Empress of India in 1876. Many Indians felt this created a special tie with Britain and the royal family often went to India.

5

The British brought their own customs and entertainments to India. They introduced cricket which became one of the national sports of India.

6

Most Indians were very poor. The cities were crowded and outbreaks of disease and famines were common. Improvements could be made only slowly.

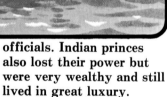

7

The two main religious groups in India were the Hindus and the Muslims. They were rivals and sometimes there were riots and people were killed.

8

The Indians had little say in how their country was ruled so a group of them formed the National Congress. At first they just wanted reforms but later they began to demand independence from Britain.

180

Convicts and Settlers

1 In 1788 the British Government began to send criminals to Australia as a punishment. Many stayed on there after they had served their sentence.

2 Soon many other settlers arrived. Most of them wanted land where they could raise sheep and cattle. Some went in search of gold and minerals.

3 Life in Australia in the 19th century was hard and often dangerous. There were "bushrangers" (outlaws). The most famous was Ned Kelly.

4 As more settlers arrived they took land from the Aborigines (native Australians), many of whom were killed, or died of diseases brought by settlers.

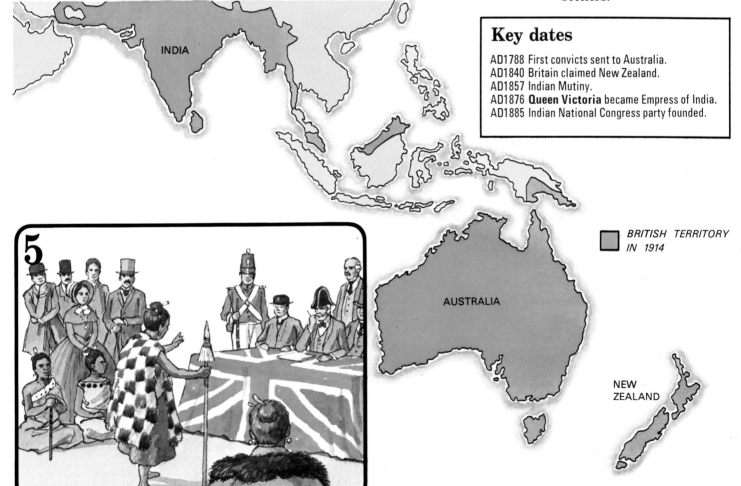

Key dates

AD1788 First convicts sent to Australia.
AD1840 Britain claimed New Zealand.
AD1857 Indian Mutiny.
AD1876 **Queen Victoria** became Empress of India.
AD1885 Indian National Congress party founded.

BRITISH TERRITORY IN 1914

5 European settlers first arrived in New Zealand in the 1790s. In 1840 the British Government took over the country. The Governor and the Maori chiefs made a treaty agreeing how much land the settlers could have, but this did not prevent fierce wars between the Maoris and the settlers.

This map shows British territory in India, South-East Asia, and Australia in 1914. By this time Australia and New Zealand had gained the right to rule themselves but they were still part of the British Empire.

Indians and Settlers

Many tribes of Indians lived in North America, each with its own way of life and language. The Indians of the Great Plains lived by farming until they captured horses from the Spaniards in the 16th century. Then most of them became nomads, hunting buffalo across the Plains and rearing horses. They lived like this for about 200 years until European settlers moved west and took the Indians' hunting grounds for their farms.

Tepee (tent made of buffalo hide)

Buffalo hunt. The buffalo provided Indians with food, clothing and shelter.

Chiefs

Traders

Meat drying

We have removed part of this tepee wall so you can see inside.

Travois (sledge)

Medicine man

Preparing buffalo hide

The Plains Indians lived in tepees which could be packed up when the buffalo moved on. The first white men to meet the Indians were traders who sold metal goods, blankets and guns and bought buffalo hides and horses.

1 Settlers move west

As more settlers from Europe moved into the original 13 States of the United States of America, more land was needed. In 1803 the Americans bought Louisiana from the French.

Settlers began to cross the Appalachian Mountains and the Great Plains, looking for land to farm. They travelled with wagons packed with everything they needed

for their new homes, so most people, except for guards and cattle herders had to walk. It usually took many months to reach a suitable area.

The settlers made treaties with the Indians promising not to take all their land. But the treaties were soon broken when settlers wanted more land.

In 1848 gold was discovered in California. Thousands of people flocked there in the "goldrush" hoping to make fortunes.

Railways were built to link the east and west coasts. These brought more settlers to the Great Plains, leaving less and less land for the Indians.

The men who built the tracks had to be fed. They employed hunters armed with rifles who killed most of the buffalo on which the Indians had depended.

The Indians fought the settlers. The wars were bitter and both sides were cruel. The Indians won victories such as at Little Big Horn when they killed

General Custer and his men. But the settlers had more soldiers and better weapons and many Indian tribes were almost wiped out.

The Indians were left with only small areas of land called reservations. They were controlled by government agents and most were very unhappy.

The Wild West

In the United States of America, many of the people who moved westwards to the vast plains and prairies started raising cattle or growing corn. Towns, like this one, grew up to supply their needs. At first they were wild, lawless places, especially when cowboys from the ranches came into town. They brought great herds of cattle to the railway depots from which they were taken to feed the people in the cities.

Large industries and cities like New York and Chicago grew up. The first skyscrapers were built. By 1890 the United States was one of the world's most powerful industrial nations.

At first life was hard for the farmers on the plains, but soon they started using tougher crops and steel ploughs and later bought machines for harvesting and threshing. Before long they were producing vast quantities of grain which were sold all over the world.

From all over Europe poor people and people persecuted for their ideas came to the United States to start a new life. Some were lucky, but many of them ended up working in factories and living in hard conditions in the big cities.

New Countries in South America

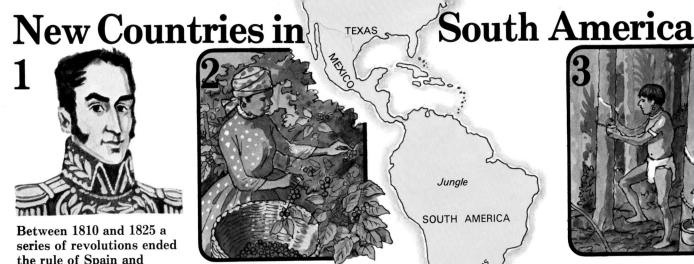

1

Between 1810 and 1825 a series of revolutions ended the rule of Spain and Portugal in South America and set up 11 new states. This is Simon Bolivar, one of the revolutionary leaders who helped to achieve this.

2

Coffee was brought from Arabia to South America and grown on large estates. By 1860 it was the main export of many states.

3

Another important export was rubber. It was made from the juice of trees growing in the Amazon jungle.

4

Many of the Indian tribes in the Amazon jungle attacked the white men who came to take over their lands.

5

On the vast pampas (grasslands) of the south-east, there were huge ranches where great herds of cattle were reared by cowboys called "gauchos".

The cattle were used for making canned meat which was sold abroad.

Mexico

1

Mexicans and Americans were always quarrelling about who should control Texas. It belonged to Mexico but many Americans had settled there and wanted to be part of the United States. Here Davy Crockett and a group of other Americans are defending the Alamo Fort against a Mexican attack.

2

In 1863 the European powers, led by France, tried to get control of Mexico by making Archduke Maximilian of Austria, Emperor of Mexico. In 1867 the Mexicans shot him.

3

From 1867 onwards the Mexicans ruled themselves. In the early 20th century civil war broke out. One of the revolutionary leaders was Pancho Villa, shown here.

Life Under the Tsars

1

The Tsars (emperors) of Russia governed their huge country from St Petersburg. There was no parliament and the Tsars and nobles, from whom they chose their ministers and officials, were very cut off from the rest of the country. Much of their time was spent at balls and receptions.

2

Most Russians were members of the Orthodox Christian Church, which supported the idea that the Tsar was chosen by God and that he alone had the right to rule.

3

Talking or writing about government reforms was forbidden. Secret police tracked down anyone suspected of wanting to change the government.

4

Many people who criticized the government for its inefficiency and cruelty, were executed or sent into exile in a part of Russia called Siberia.

5

During the 19th century there were several great novelists, playwrights and composers at work in Russia. The Russian ballet became world-famous.

6

Many Russians were serfs—peasants who lived on nobles' estates and were treated as slaves. Serfs could be bought and sold. They had to do any work their estate owner demanded and they were often given cruel punishments for small mistakes. There were frequent uprisings and riots. Eventually, in 1861, Tsar Alexander II freed the serfs. The government lent them money to buy land, but they were too poor to buy farming equipment and pay back the loans. Their lives were not much improved and some were even worse off than before.

The Crimean War

AUSTRIAN EMPIRE

RUSSIAN EMPIRE

CRIMEA

BLACK SEA

TURKISH EMPIRE

The Russians wanted to expand their empire. In the late 18th and early 19th centuries they expanded eastwards. They also won land around the Black Sea, by helping the people of these territories free themselves from the Turkish Empire. The countries of Europe were suspicious of Russia's ambitions. In 1853 Britain and France tried to capture the area called the Crimea, to stop Russian expansion. One incident in this war was the Charge of the Light Brigade (shown here). A British force misunderstood an order and charged the Russian guns.

1 Discontent grows

This is Nicholas II, who became Tsar in 1894. He was a well-meaning and kind man but he was not strong enough to be a good ruler.

2

Nicholas's wife, Alexandra, was under the spell of a monk called Rasputin. She believed he could cure her son of a blood disease, but others thought him evil.

3

Factories and industrial towns were growing up in Russia. Living conditions in the towns were very bad and many people started demanding changes.

4

In 1905 a crowd of workers went on strike and marched to the Tsar's palace to tell him their problems. Soldiers, fearing a revolution, fired on them.

5

The Tsar allowed a *Duma* (parliament) to meet for a while but then dismissed it. Meanwhile, a group of people in exile, led by Lenin, were planning a revolution.

Key dates

AD1762/1796	Reign of **Catherine the Great.**
AD1812	Invasion of Russia by Napoleon.
AD1853/1856	Crimean War.
AD1855/1881	Reign of **Alexander II.**
AD1861	Serfs freed.
AD1894/1917	Reign of **Nicholas II.**
AD1904/1905	Russia defeated in war with Japan.
AD1905	Massacre of strikers outside Tsar's palace.
AD1906	Meeting of Duma (parliament).

Western Ideas in the East

Japan

From about 1640 onwards Japan had no contact with the countries of the west, except for a few Dutch traders. Then, in 1853, Commodore Perry, the commander of a squadron of American warships, sailed to Japan and got permission for America to trade with Japan. Soon European powers followed and Japan made trade agreements with many European countries.

It was hundreds of years since any emperor of Japan had had any real power. An official called the Shogun ruled the country for the emperor. This is the last Shogun of Japan.

In 1868 the 15-year-old Emperor left the old capital, Kyoto, and set up a new one in Edo (Tokyo). Here he is arriving in Edo, where he took back power from the Shogun and set up a western-style parliament.

The small picture above shows the opening of the first parliament.

The Samurai (warriors) were replaced by a new army, trained in modern methods of fighting by advisers from France and Germany.

The Japanese learnt many other things from the west. They built railways and factories and started producing large numbers of goods quickly and cheaply.

The Japanese wanted to win power overseas. They started to interfere in China and Korea. This made them rivals with the Russians and in 1904 Japan and Russia went to war. The new, efficient Japanese army and navy quickly defeated the Russians.

1 China

Between 1644 and 1912, China was ruled by the Ch'ing (also called the Manchu) Emperors. One of the greatest was Ch'ien Lung (1736-95), shown here.

2

The Ch'ing emperors fought many wars to protect their frontiers, win more territory and put down rebellions. At first they were successful but the wars were very expensive and later emperors found it more and more difficult to pay for them. The country slowly became weaker.

3

The Chinese population was growing quickly but farming methods were still very old-fashioned. It was difficult to grow enough food for everyone.

4

The Chinese Government did not like foreigners and allowed them to trade only in certain areas. The British were keen to extend these areas and in 1839 they went to war.

5

The British won the war in 1842. They forced the Chinese to sign a treaty which gave them Hong Kong and allowed them to trade in certain other ports.

6

Some Chinese decided to strengthen China by adopting certain Western ideas and inventions, such as railways, and steamships. But many still hated foreign ideas.

7

People who hated foreigners formed a secret society called the "Boxers". In 1900 they started attacking all the foreigners they could find in China. Here they are storming a foreign embassy.

8

This is the Empress Tzu Hsi. From 1862 to 1908 she ruled China, first for her son, then for her nephew. She often plotted with those who hated foreigners.

9

In 1911 there was a revolution and the last Ch'ing Emperor was expelled from China. This is Sun Yat-sen the first President of China.

Time Chart:
Dark Ages to 1914

	North America	Central and South America	Europe	Africa
	Mound Builders living on the plains.		Gradual conversion of barbarian kingdoms to Christianity.	North Africa and Egypt part of the Byzantine Empire. North Africa and Egypt overrun by Muslim Arabs.
AD800			Invasion of Spain by Muslims. Battle of Poitiers. Muslim advance into Western Europe halted. Viking raids begin. **Charlemagne** crowned Holy Roman Emperor.	Various tribes start living south of the Sahara Desert.
AD900		Decline of Maya civilization in Mexico.		
AD1000	Vikings may have reached America.		Normans invade England. Normans invade Italy.	First Iron Age settlement at Zimbabwe.
AD1100		Chimu people living in Peru.	First Crusade.	Zimbabwe becomes a powerful kingdom.
AD1200			The Mongols invade Eastern Europe. Eighth Crusade.	Arab merchants known to be trading in West and East Africa. Rise of Empire of Mali in West Africa.
AD1300		Rise of Aztec Empire in Mexico.	Beginning of Hundred Years War. Black Death from Asia spreads through Europe.	
AD1400	People living at Huff.	Spread of Inca Empire in Peru.	First firearms developed. Invention of printing. Ideas of the Renaissance spreading from Italy.	Chinese merchants trading in East Africa. Kingdom of Benin set up.
AD1500	Voyage of Christopher Columbus.	Arrival of Spaniards. End of Aztec and Inca Empires. Arrival of Portuguese.	European explorers discover America. Beginning of Reformation. Wars of Religion between Catholic and Protestants.	Portuguese expeditions explore west coast and start trading with Africans. Turks conquered Egypt. Mali Empire destroyed. Beginning of slave trade.
AD1600	Spaniards brought horses to America. First European settlements. Pilgrim Fathers arrive in New England.		Development of trade between Europe and other parts of the world. English Civil War.	Dutch settlers arrive in South Africa.
AD1700	England wins Canada from the French. War of American Independence.		Beginning of Agricultural Revolution in Britain. Beginning of Industrial Revolution in Britain. French Revolution.	Rise of Ashanti power on west coast.
AD1800	United States buys Louisiana from the French. California goldrush. American Civil War.	Spaniards and Portuguese driven out of Central and South America. War between Mexico and United States of America.	Wars of **Napoleon** Unification of Italy. Unification of Germany.	Slave trade abolished within British Empire. The Great Trek. Opening of Suez Canal. European powers build up empires in Africa.
AD1900		Mexican Revolution begins.	World War I.	Boer war begins. Union of South Africa established.

Russia and Asia	Middle East	India	China and Japan	Far East and Pacific
Slavs in Russia.	Byzantine Empire controls much of Middle East.	India ruled by many princes.	T'ang Dynasty in China.	
Muslims conquer Persia.	Death of **Muhammad.** Spread of Muslim Empire. Muslims conquer much of Byzantine Empire.			
			Japanese capital moved to Kyoto.	
Vikings settle in Russia.				Rise of the Khmers in Cambodia. First settlers reach Easter Island and New Zealand from Polynesia.
Kiev becomes most important city in Russia.				
Russia becomes offically Christian.	Seljuk Turks invade Byzantine Empire. Invasion of Seljuk Turks.		Sung Dynasty in China.	
	The First Crusade.			
	Kingdom of Outremer founded. Life of **Saladin.**		Appearance of Samurai in Japan. Military rulers in Japan take the title "Shogun".	Large statues erected on Easter Island.
Mongols invade and conquer Russia.	Sack of Constantinople by Crusaders. End of Kingdom of Outremer.		**Marco Polo** visits China. The Mongol ruler, **Kubilai Khan,** conquers China.	
			Ming Dynasty in China.	
		Mongols invade northern India.		
Rise of Moscow. Russia gradually united. **Ivan III** becomes first Tsar and throws off Mongol power. Rise of Safavid Dynasty in Persia. **Tsar Ivan the Terrible.** Development of trade between Russia and England.	Sack of Constantinople by Ottoman Turks. End of Byzantine Empire. **Suleiman the Magnificent.** Turks threaten Europe. Turkish advance into Europe halted.	First European sea voyage to India and back, led by **Vasco da Gama** (Portuguese). Mogul Empire set up.	Long period of war in Japan. Arrival in Japan and China of European traders and missonaries.	Europeans first see Pacific Ocean. First Europeans cross Pacific Ocean on their way round the world.
Tsar Peter the Great.	Europeans try to extend their trade with Turkey and Persia.	British start regular trade with India.	All Europeans, except Dutch traders, expelled from Japan. The Manchu family start the Ch'ing Dynasty in China.	Expansion of Dutch trade in East Indies.
		British destroy French power in India.		Dutch land in Australia. **Captain Cook** reaches Australia and New Zealand. British colony of Australia founded.
Napoleon's expedition to Moscow. Crimean War. **Nicholas II** becomes Tsar.	Ottoman Empire falling apart. Russia tries to help parts of Empire break free.	Britain gradually gains control of the whole of India. Indian Mutiny. **Queen Victoria** proclaimed Empress of India.	War between the British and Chinese. **Commodore Perry** arrives in Japan.	Britain takes possession of New Zealand. French build up empire in Indo-China.
Meeting of the First Duma (parliament).	World War I.		Boxer uprising in China. War between Japan and Russia. Revolution in China. Last Ch'ing Emperor expelled.	

191

Index